*Califia Burning*
*New and Selected Poems, 1987-2020*

Tennessee Reed

# CALIFIA BURNING
## NEW AND SELECTED POEMS,
## 1987-2020

**DALKEY ARCHIVE PRESS**

McLean, IL / Dublin

CIP Data available on request.

**www.dalkeyarchive.com**
McLean, IL / Dublin

Cover Image: Betye Saar.

Printed on permanent/durable acid-free paper.

This book is dedicated to *Personal Problems'* actor, producer and family friend Walter Cotton, journalist and family friend Dori Maynard, family friend Carl Tillman, dancer and family friend Sally Gross, muralist and Berkeley City College classmate Antonio Ramos, poet and family friend Adele Foley, cousin Chaznee Nicole Brown, step-grandmother Teri LeNoir, Berkeley City College classmate Ingrid Pruitt, Arrowsmith Academy classmate Michelle Chang, fellow YMCA member Thalia Cambouroglou, family friend Ray Smith, musician Randy Weston, grandmother Ethel Snider Blank Strasser, poet Julia Vinograd, aunt-in-law Kimiko Miyazaki, family friend Andrew Hope IV, painter and family friend Joe Overstreet, writer, family friend and founder of "A Gathering of the Tribes" Steve Cannon, artist and Arrowsmith Academy art teacher Iris Polo, and writer, Pulitzer Prize Winner and family friend Toni Morrison, who all passed on during the time I was working on this book.

# Contents

# Foreword

THE POEMS IN *Califia Burning: New and Selected Poems 1987-2019*, were written between ages ten and forty-two. This foreword represents certain phases of my life, previous to writing this collection, beginning at the end of my childhood, passing through adolescence and young adulthood, and ending at the onset of peri-menopause.

My first memory of writing poetry happened when I was five years old. I was walking down the street in Oakland, California, returning home from an urgent care doctor appointment at Kaiser Hospital, for one of what seemed like endless ear infections, when I saw a spectacular rainbow arching over the city. That inspired me to write my first poem, "Thursday's Rainbow." I think this also became my first published poem, appearing in *The San Francisco Examiner* that same year, of 1982, and one of its lines became the title for my first poetry collection, *Circus in the Sky* an experiment in the then developing desktop technology, published by I. Reed Books in 1988, shortly after my eleventh birthday. I have a photograph of my mother and me editing the manuscript on her computer, organizing the old school cut and paste mock-up that became the chapbook.

The first poem in this Foreword, "The Tennessee Poem," was written when I was ten years old. It was written during the spring of 1987 when I was living in Cambridge, Massachusetts. It was also included in *Circus in the Sky*. That title not only was based on the rainbow sighting, but was likely influenced by a matching lunchbox and thermos set I used in Kindergarten, which was decorated with circus lions and elephants. If I remember correctly it also had stars and rainbows.

*The Tennessee Poem*

My name is Tennessee.
And all its people are inside of me.
My lungs are Nashville.
My heart is Chattanooga.
My veins are its rivers.
My kidneys are Memphis.
And Lookout Mountain
Is my head.

1987


For a writer, I couldn't have been luckier in the parents department. My father, Ishmael Reed, is one of the world's most gifted writers and teachers of writing. His students—many of whom have become published writers, editors and teachers—are encouraged to maintain their own voices. He just helps them get stronger. As with all of his students, he has always encouraged my work, and continued to tutor me in the writing craft and business up to the present, by having me accompany him to teaching jobs and readings, acting as his assistant, booking engagements, and managing his online magazine, *Konch*. My mother, Carla Blank, has helped young people write their own scripts for original theater works for more than forty years, so she is good at picking up on lines that work. When I first began to write, I would speak out my lines as she wrote them down, and she would help me if editing was needed. Around my mid-thirties, people would ask me "Who is the better writer, you or your dad?" It always seemed a silly question to me, but my stock answer was "We write differently," which is the truth.

Shortly after *Circus in the Sky* was published I won first place in the City of Berkeley's In Dulci Jubilo poetry contest, where I received my award in Berkeley City Hall's official Council chambers. Another amazing "endorsement" came from an astronaut, although I'm not sure now if it was Walter Shirra or another astronaut who published a book around 1988. He was waiting to make a presentation at the American Book Sellers Association meetings that May, while completed a reading of *Circus in the Sky*. He said with a big smile as we crossed paths to and from the podium, something to the effect of "I've been in the sky, too."

"Body Scape" was written in the spring of 1988 and "The W Poem" was written between the summers of 1988 and 1989, a very creative time in my life—probably because it was my preteen years, when my body was changing rapidly. I was eleven and twelve. I again won first place in the City of Berkeley's In Dulci Jublio poetry contest. Also, "The W Poem" earned me my first paycheck for writing when it was published in *Elements of Literature: First Course, Grade 7*, Texas: Holt, Reinhart and Winston, 1993. My father suggested I frame the check, which I did. It hung on my bedroom wall above my desk for years, but I am not sure where it is now.

*Body Scape*

I've been 12 years around the sun
and seen 12 winters, 12 springs,
12 summers, 12 falls.
I have spun around the earth's axis 4,380 times
and watched a new moon rise 156 times

I live in the Universe
as part of the Milky Way galaxy
between the Arctic Circle and the Tropic of Cancer
in the Western Hemisphere
about 122 degrees latitude
and about 38 degrees longitude

on the North American continent
on the West Coast of the USA
in the state of California
by the San Francisco Bay
in the county of Alameda
in the city of Oakland.

I stand with about 206 bones.
I move with about 656 muscles.
I think with 14,000,000,000 brain cells.
I taste with 9,000 taste buds
and chew with 32 grown-up teeth.
17 muscles will help me smile
and 43 muscles will help me frown.
Every 27 days I wear a new layer of skin.

I live about 26 million miles from Venus
and about 49 million miles from Mars.
When I look in my Tasco telescope to see them
they look like the mobile I watch on the ceiling.
Venus is pink and black
and Mars is gold.

When I went to sleep in Martinique
all my friends in California were in school.
When I eat breakfast in California
it's dinnertime in Zimbabwe.
When it's wintertime in Alaska,
it's summertime in Chile
and when it's summertime in Iceland
it's wintertime in Australia.

It feels like there's no time at all
when I've flown over the clouds
and the sun

even the moon.
I've seen a rainbow circle a cloud
and arch a volcano.

1988


*The W Poem*


Wednesdays are my favorite days
because they start with a W
and Wednesdays are the middle
of the week and
I like the middle.

I started liking Wednesdays
about eight or seven years ago
and I never changed
from my favorite day.

Wednesday is the poet's day
because the Roman god of the middle of the week
is Mercury, a poet's god
and the German god of the middle of the week
is Woden, a poet's god.

Wednesday's from water I think
because water starts with a W
and Woden is a rain storm god.
I think Woden likes to sing a lot
The rain songs: drip drop drip drop drip drop drip drop
and I'm Pisces the fish
and I like to swim a lot.

The Greeks had no W.
The Latins had no W.
The English had a W since 1066.
They got it from the Germans.
It's a double V
so why is it called a double U?
I think because the shape of the character
was invented from two U's.

I like the W words: win, won, wood, wet.
          west, well, wear,
               water and Washington

I wish everyday was Wednesday
because, although I like Fridays sometimes,
I like some space on either side
of my week.
It makes me feel warm,
like having two friends
sitting with me.

1988, 1989


The poem "Electric Chocolate," which was the title poem for my second poetry collection, was also written in the summer of 1989. I was twelve years old and in-between sixth and seventh grades, inspired by a huge Hershey's chocolate bar wrapper in the form of a banner I found along one wall of my bedroom in the home of the poet Heather McHugh, which my parents had rented while teaching in the summer session at the University of Washington, Seattle. Heather McHugh graciously gifted me the banner, upon learning of my poem. *Electric Chocolate* was published in 1990 by Raven's Bones Press, located in Sitka, Alaska, run by our family friend, the late Tlingit poet Andrew Hope III. I was thirteen and in-between seventh and eighth grades.

*Electric Chocolate*

First Piece

I like Hershey's chocolate
bars because they are
rich and creamy. I imagine
that the tree in our front
yard is growing Hershey's.
The telephone poles and wires
are made of Hershey's. I
pretend I go out and
pick them off the tree. The
poles are chocolate wood.
The wires are electric chocolate.
Hershey's milk chocolate bars.

Second Piece

I wish I saw Hershey's everywhere
I wish my house was made of Hershey's
I wish I slept in a Hershey's bed
I wish I swam in chocolate water
I wish I was made of chocolate water
I wish this was Hershey's writing
I wish the world was made of Hershey's

1989

Some psychologists have suggested that my poems, representing
nearly forty years in the evolution of my thinking, offer a clear
example for study of the developing brain at different stages
of life. If you are interested in what could be in the mind of a
thirteen-year-old middle school student, take a look at "New
Year's Resolution," which was written at the end of 1990/the

beginning of 1991. "Washington, D.C." was an assignment for my ninth grade English class, written in the spring of 1992, after my first trip there, which occurred during the time of the Anita Hill/Clarence Thomas hearings. We saw the crowd gathered in front of the Supreme Court, loudly chanting. I was fifteen and beginning to understand the dynamics of American style power.

*New Year's Resolution, 1991*

I want to go
to Germany and Czechoslovakia this year
at least those two countries
and all over Central
and Eastern Europe
and go back to Pittsburgh
to swill at JCC
and to Southern California
and Echo Lake Environmental Camp
(except for the backpacking trip)
again.

I want to get
a whole lot more
jean skirts
and jean jackets
to go with them—
to get a whole bunch of clothes
and let my hair grow.

I want to see
the whole body
put together—
what real people's
arteries and veins look like—
the color
and stuff.

I want to get
my children's book
published.

I would like
to dye my hair black
No,
make that blonde.

I would like to move
to the East Coast
Philadelphia, Pennsylvania
and Cambridge, Massachusetts.

I would like to be
M.C. Hammer,
Winona Rider,
to join the Ice Capades,
to be on one music video
in a song I like.

1990, 1991


*Washington, D.C.*

Home of the nation's
business. Home of the laws
and the Congress. Home
of the New World Order.
Home of the great airports
Dulles International and Washington
National. Founded by George
Washington and the permission
of Maryland to take its land.
Home of the Kitty Hawk the

Wright Brothers flew located
at the National Air and Space
Museum. Washington. District of
Columbia.

You can get a Pecan Pie at the
Holiday Inn. You can sit in a
taxi with a T.V. in the front
going to the airport. You can
get Merry-Go-Round rides at
the park across the street from
the Smithsonian gift shop.
You can fly in and out of the
airports every hour. Washington
District of Columbia.
You can buy a Congressman's votes.

1992

Shortly after I wrote "Washington, D.C." I traveled to Germany
where I read at the University of Potsdam under an arts program
of the United States Information Agency. I was the youngest per-
son ever to participate in that program that I believe no longer
exists. 1992 was the same year that my poems, "The Old Parents
Blues" and "Three Heavens and Hells" were set to music by two
composers, Carman Moore and Meredith Monk, respectively.
They were premiered during a collaboration with the Children's
Troupe of Roberts & Blank, for an Oakland dance festival in
which I was a performer. Later on, in 1998, I took a bow—
with conductor Michael Tilson Thomas, Meredith Monk and
her ensemble—on the Davies Hall stage of the San Francisco
Symphony when they performed "Three Heavens and Hells" as
part of a New Music festival.

The fall of 1992 was very difficult. The day after I started
tenth grade, September 10, my mother mysteriously got sick and

after a week of tests had to have emergency surgery. Fortunately, she made it. At that same time I found out that I was severely allergic to sulfur based antibiotics. I was given them for an ear infection. Then, on November 6, my cousin died in a car crash. She was going to turn nineteen at the end of December of 1992. She was a freshman at Hampton University in Virginia where she was studying pre-Med.

*Today, Sunday*

Today, Sunday
the twenty-seventh of December,
was supposed to
be Marquel's birthday.

The weather fit the day:
gray, gloomy, cold;
Marquel was supposed
to be nineteen.

She died November 6, 1992
in a car accident.
This was in Hampton, Virginia
where she was a freshman
pre-Med student in college.

There were 4 passengers in the car
when the driver fell asleep
and the car crashed into a tree.
The other 4 lived;
but Marquel died.

We can't say whose fault it was,
but the driver must feel
really scared and guilty.

I remember the day of the funeral.
We went into the Oakland hills,
trying to find the Church.
Instead, we found burnt down houses.

When we found Lake Temescal,
we knew we were going the right way.
The Church was so crowded
we had to stand up for a long time.

When her best friend spoke about her
and began to cry,
I started to cry.

We got lost
two more times that day.
We went straight
from school to her house,
going down Thornhill
trying to find Mountain Boulevard
and going up and down Snake Road
onto Manzanita Drive.

We watched *Cinderella*
with two kids,
Marquel's cousins,
named Brianna and Jordan.
I talked to them
and ate dinner.
Then we drove back home.

Now when I work
at my Uncle's doctor office,
she won't be there
typing on the computer

and talking on the phone.
It will be so weird.

1993


After all of this was over things turned around for the better. Right after I finished tenth grade, my best and favorite year in high school, I read my poetry in an international poetry festival at The Hague and Eindhoven, the Netherlands.

I read my poetry again in Germany, in 1994, at Bonn's American High School and at the John F. Kennedy High School in Berlin, arranged by the same U.S. Department of State program as in my first trip. I was a senior in high school.

"Pact With the Devil" was written in 1995 and I was about to turn eighteen. It was inspired by a reading assignment during my twelfth grade American Literature course, probably a short story by Nathaniel Hawthorne, although now I forget exactly which one. This was during my second creative writing spurt, the years of 1995 and 1996, when I was moving on from high school to college and transitioning to adulthood.

*Pact with the Devil*

I walked through the woods
leaving my life in the town behind
I was afraid of the dark
and the tight space
afraid of the unknown

I walked with my friends
we were all African American
runaway slaves
women who wanted to be free
of Baltimore's grasp

so we followed the call of our husbands
who had taken the journey
to Canada
before us

Everywhere was woods then
there was no escape from trees
we had to pass
through the woods
called the Devil's woods
as we headed North through Buffalo
to Canada

We believed in the Devil
a white slavemaster who lived in the trees
with big eyes and a laughing red face

We knew
the Devil followed us
through his woods
because he lighted our way with his gleaming red eyes
and cleared a trail with his arrow-shaped tail

The woods were endless
so we needed rest
and a way
to stay inside
because the cold had come
and we could travel
no further

We all agreed
with the Devil
to give up our souls
for a cabin of wooden logs
something that was part

of the Devil
for something that was part
of us

So we rested in the cabin
and warmed our forgotten souls
until a while later
when a fierce white man
on a wild white horse appeared
at our door

He dragged us to where the Devil
was that was part of him—
that was his own wood—
and now he wanted it back
to feel complete

But we weren't ready to give him the wood back
because it was still winter
time and the cold
kept us
wanting to be
inside

He pointed to thundery clouds
at flashes of lightning
and the crack of thunder

The lightning flashed face
of our husbands
their faces and beards
extending out as the North Wind
calling to us
this would be our fate, too

We ran back
Into the log house
which disintegrated
turning us invisible
the moment we reentered
the Devil's space

We whirled up to the clouds
joining the North Wind
traveling Northwest
strangely, still
following the route
we had set to Canada

Our bodies flew up in the sky
but our souls remained on the ground
routed forever
in the Devil's woods

This story took place in Baltimore
during the 1860's
I can tell this tale
because I was once
one of these women
heading toward Buffalo
to escape through
Niagara Fall
to Canada

1995

It is no secret that I love to travel, especially by airplanes. I have
studied airlines, their routes, hubs and safety records so long
and so seriously that friends ask me to advise them on the best
flights to book. I can still recite the flight numbers, dates of
travel, airports and times of departure and landing for trips we

made even ten, twenty, thirty years ago, which can prove handy, for instance, around tax time or when writing autobiographies. "The Study of a Young, Smiling Flight Attendant" and "Nihon No Ryokō" were both written in the summer of 1996 when I was nineteen years old and between my first and second years of college, after I had the great experience of traveling in Japan as arranged by the U.S. Department of State. On that trip I read at the University of Sapporo. These were all included in my third poetry collection, Airborne, which was published in 1996, again by Raven's Bones Press. I was in my second year of college.

*The Story of a Young, Smiling Flight Attendant*

In an American Airlines ad
that appears on CNN
A young flight attendant
walks down the gateway.
With a curious frown,
she's looking at airplanes
parked at the gates.
She is like the woman
in *Portrait of Victorine Meurent*
by the painter Edouard Manet.

The plane takes off.
It's a DC-10.

Segue to inside the cabin.
A little girl kneels in her mom's lap,
held close and tight
as she looks over the back of a seat.
The mother and daughter are right out of
*Madonna of the Chair* by Raphael.
Her mother is pointing at something
as they sit and talk
by the window.

The young flight attendant appears again
smiling at all the passengers
like the woman in Pontormo's
*Portrait of a Young Woman.*

Segue to outside, in a heavenly blue sky.
The American Airlines plane is flying,
like the angel in *A Maiden's Dream*,
like Lorenzo Lotto.

Segue again to the plane's interior.
A man and a woman
holding hands
like *The Arnolfini Marriage* by Jan Van Eyck.
The flight attendant is smiling at them
like the woman in *The Magdalen* by
Bernadino Luini.

The screen turns black.
Ad copy rolls in white
as a piano continues to play
the advertising jingle.

I wish I'd met this flight attendant
with her inviting smile
who fooled me into thinking
I would find her in real life.

I found her in a movie,
called *Baby's Day Out.*
She played a mother
looking for her baby
who had memorized the images
in a book
and traveled
all over town

looking for the images
just like I traveled
over four centuries
to find images
in the world's museums
that matched
that perfect world.

1996


*Nihon No Ryokō*
*(Japanese Travel)*

You can't always take the airline
you want to take like American or TWA
sometimes you have to take whatever's cheaper
like United or Northwest

You can't always
sit by the window
on the airplane
sometimes you have to sit
by the aisle or
in the middle

You can't always get
American food
like hamburgers, pizza
eggs, and ham
sometimes you can
only eat Japanese food like
sushi, teriyaki, sunomono, and chawanmushi

You can't stay in one place
all of the time

sometimes you have to Shinkansen to or from
a new city daily
like Osaka or Tokyo

You can't always find clunky heeled loafer
Japanese school girl shoes
in your size in Kobe or Kyoto
sometimes you have to go to Nagoya
to find them

You can't always rely on following the schedule
like when I was told
we would go exploring in the morning
or eat at a certain restaurant
sometimes you have to accept
last minute changes like when our guide decided to choose
a restaurant where we sat on tatami mats
instead of a Chinese restaurant
where we could sit on chairs, like at home

You can't get a hotel room
with a big space like the Rihga Royal in Hiroshima
you sometimes have to stay in a tiny
hole-in-the-wall
like the Personal Hotel
in Fukuoka, where the price is good

You won't find the U.S.
everywhere
but you will find courteous people everywhere
safe streets and subways at night
full of people having fun
the walking signal on traffic lights
        playing "Coming Through the Rye"
and 1001 golden visions at Sanjusangendo
moats surrounding the walls of Nijo Castle

red, yellow, or white triangles
    on selected windows
    of high rise glass skyscrapers
the mixture of gray rock, raked granite
    and luscious green gardens
    at the Silver Pavilion
the stork, with his beak striped in pastels
    like a Richard Diebenkorn painting
as he stares from a rock at the Miyajima Aquarium
and a herd of deer following you, asking to be fed
on the beach at the Itsukushima Shrine

1996


I wrote "Choosing Sides" in the fall of 1998 after I had just transferred from Laney College and begun my junior year at the University of California at Berkeley. This was during a lengthy hiatus from writing poetry, because I was concentrating on writing my memoir, *Spell Alburquerque: Memoirs of a 'Difficult' Student* (CounterPunch/AK Press, 2009). That prose project went through many changes over the twelve years it took to complete. "Choosing Sides" shows me at twenty-one years, still trying to figure out who I was. It was published in *The San Francisco Chronicle* that fall.

*Choosing Sides*

In America
everybody belongs to one team
and people like me
are always asked to choose sides

Every day I feel
like I'm trying out for something
because people put pressure on me

to choose one race
or one religion
or to join them in their cause

Black people say to me
"Your father is Black?
I don't see any Black in you."
White people say to me,
"You have Russian, Irish,
French, Danish and Scottish?
You look Mexican, Indian,
Black and Asian."
Native Americans say to me,
"You look Mexican,
Black and White to me. You
don't look Cherokee."
Asians say to me, "Your
Mother has some Asian ancestors?
I would have never guessed."
Latinos and Chicanos
are disappointed when they ask me,
"Habla español?"
and I reply, "Un poquito."

People tell me that my parents
should have thought of this
before they had me
because as one woman put it,
"God says that Blacks should marry Blacks,
and Whites should marry Whites.
Christians should marry Christians
and Jews should marry Jews."
(I can't find that quote in the Bible)

1998

"The City Beautiful" was written two years later, in the fall of 2000, following my research for a paper on San Francisco's City Hall, one of my favorite buildings, and the City Beautiful Movement. I was twenty-three and in my senior year at U.C. Berkeley. It was also published in *The San Francisco Chronicle*.

*The City Beautiful*

Five hundred feet high
and five hundred thousand square feet wide
of polished brass, marble, wrought iron
carved stone and Manchurian wood
City Hall towers over San Francisco's Civic Center
with 24-karat gold leaf shimmering on its dome
while homeless citizens
shuffle around the public library
and the Civic Center BART station
in muddy blue jeans and black sweatshirts
dappled with pigeon droppings

Workers rush from BART and the MUNI metro
and climb the grand marble rotunda staircase
to their City Hall offices
in their expensive DKNY and Ralph Lauren suits
while homeless people push all their belongings
in shopping carts
and talk about buying booze at the convenience store
in the corner of Market and Eighth Streets

Students catch elevators to the History Room
at the San Francisco Public Library
while security officers harass homeless women
trying to use the restroom

Parents and children
dressed up to see "The Nutcracker"

at the War Memorial Opera House
another fancy marble, gold, and red velvet confection
pass by homeless people sitting on rotting wood benches
in the United Nations Plaza
freezing and wet from the rain

At City Hall's opening day ceremony
protesters shouted, "Food, not gold leaf."

2000

"The Oakland Hills Fire, 1991" and "Disney's Cinderella" were written while I participated in my father's poetry workshop, the summer of 2002, at the Atlantic Center for the Arts in New Smyrna Beach, Florida. I was twenty-five. He had given the workshop participants an assignment to write a poem about a hero or shero. "Disney's Cinderella" was published in an anthology edited by Ishmael Reed, entitled *From Totems to Hip Hop: A Multicultural Anthology of Poetry Across the Americas, 1900-2002* (Thunder's Mouth Press, 2003).

*Oakland Hills Fire, 1991*

Temperature ninety degrees
winds forty miles per hour
humidity ten percent

I go up on my back porch roof
and look out at the hills
through my telescope
Thick black smoke
fills the afternoon sky
red highlights flash
It's a very dry heat

The fire starts rolling
down the hill towards us
We are told to evacuate
if it reaches the flats
where we live
Mom packs emergency
clothing, blankets, food,
computer disks, family photos
and a flashlight in a box
Dad just wants
to spare the TV

Dad and I decide to go
check on our elderly neighbor,
Mrs. Johnson
Her rose garden
is the pride of the block
She is eighty-nine years old
and can climb a flight of stairs
without wheezing
Jesus is her roommate

The fire halts at the Claremont Hotel
awed by its turrets and lace-like beauty

Our friend, Eloisa
lost her house
She showed us
her gold and silver necklaces
bracelets, and brooches
melted into a sudden clump
the only treasure left of our beloved home
The house of another friend, Nancy
was spared because her son David
climbed on the roof and kept spraying with water
The flames lightly touched their garden wall

My Uncle Michael
and Aunt Denise were also spared
The fire couldn't leap over the rim of the Oakland hills
to reach their house just down the way on the other side

Some people weren't lucky
They died in their cars
trapped, trying to escape
down congested, narrow roads

We could smell the fire for days
It reeked of burnt rubber and wood
this landscape of gray ash
dotted with occasional chimneys
and stairways to nothing

Ten and a half years later
almost all the lots are reclaimed
the roads remain too narrow
The houses are now
twice as large as the old ones were
and sit even closer together

2002


*Disney's Cinderella*

She would wake up every morning
to an evil stepmother and jealous stepsisters
She was treated like a slave,
doing the cooking and cleaning
Her stepmother always complained about her food:
"Cinderella, the pasta is too sticky,
and the salad has ice burn"
or "Cinderella, the potatoes are a bit too hard"

Then Cinderella was ordered to make their dinner again
One of the stepsisters accused her or stealing
her dark blue boot-cut jeans
and white cotton blouse by Guess
The other stepsister accused
her of driving her Chevy Cavalier
without asking her
when she went to pick up Ivory Soap
at Duane Reade
(It turns out that her stepsister's ugly
boyfriend had borrowed it)
Her punishment was to go upstairs
to her stepmother's room
to hear a long list of new chores
like changing her new baby stepsister's
Pampers Baby Dry disposable diaper
and cleaning the kitchen with Clorox wipes
and wiping down the bathroom with Windex and Pinesol
Despite all of this, Cinderella was an upbeat young woman
She did what she was told, and she was very pleasant

There were times when Cinderella would give up
like where her animal friends had made
her a dress for the prince's ball
that was superior to Versace and Miyake
and it was ripped apart by her stepsisters
There were other times when she would
lose her temper or her patience
like when her name was called every two seconds
"Cinderella, it's Tuesday night, take out the garbage,"
or "Cinderella the hamper is full"
She had her animals in her corner
like her mice, her dog, horses and birds
as well as her Fairy Godmother

Because of the Fairy Godmother's storied enchantment
Cinderella was able to attend the ball
which was RSVP only
It was held at the Pierre Hotel
and Peter Duchin's band performed
The prince had his eye on her
even though there were hundreds in the room
including her stepsisters who had crashed the gate
One was eating Krispy Kreme doughnuts
even though she was diabetic
The other was eating
a big bag of Cool Ranch Dorito chips
She licked the remainders off of her fingers
The Blue Book crowd was thinking, "How grotesque"
The prince was stunned by Cinderella's beauty
and was disappointed that she vanished
all except for her slippers
He arrived at her house in his shiny, gold Lexus
and slipped a glass shoe on her foot,
which was more fancy
than the latest shoe by Giuseppe Zanotti
They flew off in his private Lear jet
to honeymoon in Walt Disney World
and Disney's private island in the Bahamas
The angry stepsisters and mother showed up at the gate
but it was too late
The plane was taxiing out to the runway

2002, 2003


"Circus Tiger" and "City Dwellers" were written in 2003 and 2004 as part of my Mills College master's thesis, "Animals and Others." I was twenty-six and twenty-seven. All of these poems were published in *City Beautiful*, which combined my fourth/ fifth poetry collections of "City Beautiful" with a revised version

of "Animals and Others," as published in 2006 by Ishmael Reed
Publishing Company.

*Circus Tiger*

At the UniverSoul Circus
six white tigers and two Bengal tigers
sit on their haunches in an arc
surrounding the gorgeous Ameera Diamond
the first Black female animal trainer in the world
who is dressed in a gray and black tiger
striped see through tankini
and matching leggings and long, black boots

They stare at her
eyes glistening gold and aqua marine
They open their huge mouths
showing fierce, white teeth
as she flicks her whip
in front of their noses

When she ignites the hoop into a circle of fire
a white tiger cooperates
flying through the flames
but a Bengal tiger hesitates
then turns back around and jumps down
He narrows his eyes at the trainer as if to say
"Hell, no, I'm not jumping through that hoop.
Do I look like I got the word
'stupid' written across my forehead?"

Miss Diamond looks peeved
This is one of those times
she says in an interview
that he "pulled a fast one on her"
and although she looks

like she wants to whip his ass
she puts the flame out

2003


*City Dwellers*

Dad and I drive down Spruce Street in Berkeley
As Dad slams on his brakes
at the intersection of Marin Avenue
and Spruce Street
a young white-tailed deer
ears alert, sprints across the street
on long, thin legs
Dad and I watch the deer
as she makes it to the other side
and turns her head to look behind
large-eyed
before disappearing
up the Marin Avenue hill

She has excellent street smarts
unlike the common opossum
who hardly ever makes it
alive to the other side
That's why they're known as road kill
One hobbles up my back stairs
to his favorite hideout underneath the roof
trailing his long, rat-like tail
thick fur dull and gray
He isn't too fast
can't see worth a damn
and he definitely isn't that bright either
My friend Heather and I study him
in awe of his comfort

with his ugliness and stupidity
as she shares a cozy hole
under the eaves with my cat
while she licks her paws
She pretends not to notice him

Dad hears three northern raccoons
thumping around on our back porch roof
sounding like a whole army has invaded the backyard
They try to raid the garbage can
It is 11:30 at night and I am in bed
with my cat sleeping next to me
I don't hear a thing
"Get out of here! Go away!"
Dad shouts as he throws his size thirteen shoes,
cleaning products and wrapped up newspapers towards them
They all stumble away in their zigzagging short-legged way
One of them, who was bigger than my cat,
looked up at me with two glassy black eyes
a few days earlier
It was so dark I couldn't see
the huge black circles
surrounding his beady eyes
*Wow this is a big cat*, I thought
*How can a cat get that big? What did it eat to get that big?*
I don't find out it's a raccoon until my friend Rebecca says
"Oh, my God, I just saw the biggest raccoon,"
after she finished smoking a cigarette

In the morning I chase a tree squirrel
as he tries to bury his walnuts in my flower pots
He is the fastest squirrel I have ever seen
As he protects his territory from the other squirrels
in the neighborhood
he scatters dirt out of the flowerpots
to bury his walnuts

and leaves big holes where plants used to be
He scurries over the back fence
the moment I approach him
Must have been the red-breasted robin
who told him we moved his walnuts

Later on in the evening a striped skunk
comes through the cat door
and sprays musk on my dog
who smells like tomato juice and skunk
after we try to clean her up

When I tell my friends these stories
they ask me if I live in the woods

2004


The three following poems were published in my sixth poetry
collection entitled *New and Selected Poems 1982-2011*, which
was published in 2011 by World Parade Books, edited by the
publisher, Paul Tayyar. "Roses for Rose Street" was written in the
spring of 2008 and was published in *Berkeleyside* Magazine. At
that time, Berkeley's Rose Street was an obsession for me. Every
time I visited that side of town I had to check if any changes
were going on there. I was thirty-one.

*Roses for Rose Street*

Leaving Berkeley Horticultural Nursery
we turned left on Rose Street
heading towards Shattuck Place
Our destination: Safeway
in the Gourmet Ghetto neighborhood
where Rose and Shattuck Place meet
I had never noticed roses on Rose Street

until that day
Before I had just paid attention
to the Japanese red maple trees
lined up in front of homes
with many types of flowering bushes
planted on the edges of lawns
in front of living room windows
between McGee Avenue and California Street

I was thinking about how Rose Street got his name
as we pass by a house
with an all yellow hybrid tea rose bush
signs of platonic or dying love
in front of a house between Grant Street and Edith Street
I thought about the song "Yellow Rose of Texas"
that I learned about from a friend
at work who is from the Dallas area
and whose work brought her a dozen yellow roses
as a thank you gift
"There's a yellow rose in Texas, that I'm going to see.
Nobody else could miss her, not half as much as me.
She cried so when I left her, it'd like to broke my heart,
And if I ever find her, I nevermore will part."

Then I saw a large shingled house
between Josephine Street and Grant Street
with a large light pink hybrid tea rose
a sign of sympathy and admiration
Now when we pass by
I check for the large, bald eagle
painted under the roof on the Josephine Street side of the
house
and the painted squirrel on the Rose Street side
and red and green jalapeño peppers
The house is a Western stick style house
a sign of the Arts and Crafts Movement

In between Milvia Street and Bonita Avenue
I saw many climbing roses in front of homes
in a variety of different colors: red, pink, yellow and white

At the Men's Faculty Club on the U.C. Berkeley Campus
where we celebrated Mom's birthday
I asked a longtime family friend, John Roberts
who is a landscape architect
how Rose Street got its name
He replied that the developers named it
after they killed the roses
in order to build the street

2007, 2008


"Jackson's Soundtrack" was written in 2009/2010 shortly after Michael Jackson died. I was thirty-two and thirty-three. I have performed it with bands backing me up at SF Jazz Center, Yoshi's and The Jazz School in Basel, Switzerland.

*Jackson Soundtrack*

I am five years old
and in Kindergarten
Michael Jackson's *Thriller*
has just come out
The song I remember most is "Beat It"
Alex Maynard, the son of the late Bob Maynard
and the late Nancy Hicks Maynard
has just turned three
I remember him dancing around the house
singing "Beat It, Just Beat It"

Five years later
I am now in fifth grade

The Children's Troupe
of Robert's & Blank is warming up
for our rehearsal of "joE"
We dance to "Man in the Mirror"
from Michael Jackson's album *Bad*
My friend Niecy,
who is sick of hearing the song,
says "Oh, Lordy Jesus"
which receives laughter from her friends
We have been dancing to "Man in the Mirror"
for a few weeks now

Another five years later
I am now fifteen
and wrapping up my ninth grade year
We are in Germany
In Nuremberg's Altstadt or old town
we walk towards a restaurant
All of a sudden "Black or White"
from Michael Jackson's album *Dangerous* blasts
We all turn our attention
A crowd has gathered around an outdoor stage
A Black model and a White model
starts dancing in black and white
striped short-sleeved sweaters,
short white knit shorts,
white crew socks and black sneakers
We stop for a second to watch the show
in this town where the Nuremberg Trials took place

On the same trip
we are traveling home
on a Swissair Boeing 747-400
that is traveling from Geneva to Los Angeles
"Keep It In The Closet" also from *Dangerous*
is playing on one of the audio channels

It is two years later
June of 1994
I am now seventeen
and it is the summer before
my senior year in high school
Dad and I are traveling
on American Airlines Flight #14
a red eye DC-10 jet traveling between
Honolulu and Los Angeles
I am not able to sleep with a crying toddler
a few rows up
and a movie blaring in my eyes
I listen to "Human Nature"
my favorite song by Michael Jackson
from his album *Thriller*

Again two years later
June of 1996
I am nineteen
We are now in Japan
and traveling on the bullet train
between Tokyo and Kyoto
We are the beginning of our Japanese tour
I am listening to "You Are Not Alone"
on a compilation CD I have
*1996 Grammy Nominees*
Fuji-san flashes by

It is now four years later
August of 2000
I am twenty-three
I have just returned home
from studying abroad in Luton, England
for two and a half months
and I am about to enter my senior year of college
at the University of California at Berkeley

"ABC" from Michael Jackson's album ABC
plays in the background of a commercial
for Old Navy's graphic tees
I go to Old Navy
and buy a couple of graphic tees

It is now July of 2002
I am now twenty-five
AmeriCorps is having
its end of the year retreat
at the Marin Headlands
The theme of the evening dance
is 80s music
"Billie Jean" is one of the songs that is played
I put my *Thriller* CD in my suitcase three weeks later
to bring down to the Atlantic Center for the Arts
in New Smyrna Beach, Florida to listen to
Once I am down there I do my exercises to it
on the living room floor
in the master artists' cottage made of pinewood
I also listen to it walking in between
the cottage and my workshop
on the wooden boardwalk that keeps us separated
from the snakes, alligators, the armadillo and the tortoise
that makes the Atlantic Center their home

Even though he has died
his soundtrack, so significant in my life,
continues

2009, 2010

"For Boadiba" was written in 2010, after listening to my poet
friend Boadiba recount her experiences during the earthquake
in Haiti, which happened while she was visiting her family in

Pétion-ville, a suburb of Port-au-Prince. I was about to turn
thirty-three.

*For Boadiba*

January 12, 2010 a 7.0 earthquake hits Haiti
I worry about whether my friend Boadiba
is dead under the rubble
or whether she is injured or sick
I have images of her sleeping in the streets
with no food, with only the clothes on her back
I wonder if she would be able to come out of Haiti
or if she will be stuck down there
limbs sticking out of a building's foundation
trapped in an elevator
fallen through a hole in the streets
killed by a looter
kidnapped by the Tonton
trampled by the fleeing crowds
stranded in a place where no one can hear her
dehydrated from lack of water
or at the business end of an American bayonet
whether she has an infected wound or broken leg
in a place where there is no anesthesia

Finally I hear from her
She says she's okay
The house "rocked like a boat," she says
but it didn't fall
She is with her sister
in the hills above the suburb of Pétion-ville
located east of the city
She slept two nights in the driveway
but returned to the house
for fear of being kidnapped
by the prisoners who tried

to kidnap her sister the year before
They got out of jail because of the earthquake
and are roaming the streets

My friend's knee is injured making her immobile
and making it difficult for her to ride in a car
Her sister volunteers in a Port au Prince hospital
while Boadiba recuperates in the house
"I came to Haiti to relax and go to the beach
and get a tan," she tells me
"But I got an earthquake instead"

She tells me that the huge, bear like dogs
that her brother owns didn't need a warning
They jumped up and ran
like the golden lab before
the earthquake hit Eureka
and my deceased cat Happy
who acted strangely
while the neighborhood dogs
barked for a week
before the Loma Prieta quake hit
They don't need to debate global warming
They just move north

Boadiba did not see the people in the slums
but she hears the stories from her sister and friends
They say that people are camped out on blankets
irritated at the news cameras stuck in their faces
I see newsreels and photographs
of a woman feeding her infant daughter baby food
She glares at the CNN camera
A group of men with poker faces
stand against a fence
They throw things at the camera
Another American invasion

I see people being treated
for injuries and illnesses
by Cuban doctors in medical tents
A small boy with a large bandage
wrapped around his head
looks curiously at the camera
while he sucks on two fingers
He is sitting in his mother's lap
A teenage girl lies in a hospital bed
and talks to her doctors in French
after they amputate her leg
She smiles at them
Before the cameras are packed up
and the media moves onto another story
their philosophy "If it bleeds, it leads,"
much attention is given to the fate
of White missionaries
instead of the thousands of Haitians
dying in buildings

Boadiba went for a vacation
She thought she'd lay on the beach
or read a book in bed
She produced an earthquake diary instead

2010

"For Wella" was also written in 2010, which I first read during the mass marking the one-year anniversary of the passing of my friend Elisa Miranda's mother, Visitacion Miranda. I was thirty-three.

*For Wella*

I remember watching the 1994 movie
"It Could Happen to You"
starring Nicolas Cage and Bridget Fonda
Wella had it on videotape
I laughed at the scene
where Bridget Fonda and Nicolas Cage
roller-skate in Central Park
Nicolas Cage landed in the pond
Wella looked at me and smiled

The Spanish soaps played
on Wella's television set
in the living room of her small home
She is from Puerto Rico originally
Wella, mother of eight
was sitting in her easy chair
in her white robe with the dark pink roses
Her late son Poly was sitting in a chair to the left
and laughing at the confrontation
between two young ladies
Her youngest son Carlos
was sitting on the rose patterned couch
The window behind him faced the street
Rosa her granddaughter
and longtime family friend
was in the kitchen preparing to serve
the Chinese takeout dinner with me
Beef and broccoli,
chicken fried rice and pot stickers
Pictures of Wella's children,
grandchildren and great-grandchildren
were framed on the alter with candles
A framed portrait of Wella as a young woman
hung in the center above the altar

I remember her voice when I called
"Hello?" she answered
"Is Elisa there?" I asked
"Ivette, it's Tennessee" I hear her say
Those are the two last words
I will ever hear her say

On Manhattan's Lower East Side
I saw two Nuyorican women in the supermarket
that look like they could be Wella's twins
I do a double take
I had two dreams about her:
one in Miami
where she was in Elba's living room
talking with Elba and Elisa
Her voice was clear
Wella the puppy is sitting in my lap
Another dream was in New York
Wella was in the apartment
my parents and I were subletting
Wella told me to take care of Rosa and Elisa

Every time I see
the United Airlines hangar at SFO
as we head down US 101 south of San Bruno
or to the airport
I think about Wella
as the hangar was my way of knowing
that we were almost at Wella's

2010


Six months after *New and Selected Poems 1982-2011* came out
I conducted poetry workshops and readings with Palestinian
high school and college students all over East Jerusalem under

an arts program of the United States Department of State. It was 2012 and around the time we arrived a flair-up in the hostilities between Palestinians and Israelis was occurring, after four Americans were assassinated in Libya, so bodyguards were assigned to accompany me on my appearances. Because of these experiences, my first in the Middle East, and as I have continued to remain in touch with students I met there, I can better understand how the Palestinians and Israelis remain in such a state of unresolved tension.

The new poems that follow this Foreword were written between 2012 and 2019 (ages thirty-five to forty-two). They continue addressing the obsessions that have appeared in all my collections: animals wild and tame; natural disasters; travel to new places; my wardrobe and hairdo choices; and the health particulars of my friends and myself. Convalescing from various back procedures proved to motivate another writing inspiration wave, as did a diagnosis of pre-diabetes, entering my forties, and the onset of peri-menopause. And writing continues to be my way to express my concerns for the precarious state of our nation and the world.

While working on this manuscript I read some of these poems in engagements around the United States and in Europe, with some poems premiering at poetry festivals and conferences. "How High the Moon" premiered at the SF Jazz Poetry Festival in 2014. "Like an Old Friend Whom You Had Given Up for Dead Rain Returns to Oakland," "Grand Duchess and Duke," and "Earth's Black Hole" premiered in Switzerland at the Kantonsschule Olten and the Jazz School in Basel in 2015. "Why No Flowers for Africa?" premiered at the Ca' Foscari University of Venice in Italy, and I read it at the Comune Sal Verde in Treviso, Italy and at the Palazzo Leoni Montanari in Vicenza, Italy in 2016. Ca' Foscari University students translated this poem into Italian, and it was published in both Italian and English in *una bussola per l'inforsfera* edited by Nicola Paladin and Giogio Rimondi (Agenzia X, 2017). I also read some of these poems at the Llibreria Calders, a bookstore in Barcelona in 2018.

To borrow from a saying, it takes an international village to make a poet....! I thank all the people who have helped me along the way.

# Introduction
## Lamont B. Steptoe

CALIFORNIA MIGHT BE burning but so is the passion of poet Tennessee Reed! Zora Neale Hurston said, "You gotta go there to know there!" Tennessee Reed has gone there and knows there! One is amazed not only by her memory of things back-in-the-day but also how detailed these memories are. Let me remind you, we are speaking of a poet who had her first book published at the age of eleven. Reed takes on many of the hot topics of our day, i.e. racism, sexism, globalization, climate change, gentrification, war in the Middle East, the West's overlooking of African people's humanity. However, as serious as these issues may be, Reed also has an open heart that allows her to maintain a sense of a humor, a sense of wonder, a sense of hope, a sense of playfulness. In one poem, she's a plantain, in another a blood orange, in another a Brussels Sprout, in another a strawberry while in yet another she's a bobcat. Let's check out an example:

I immigrated to the U.S.
from my birthplace,
Brussels, Belgium,
where I lived
since 1587
taking the long journey
to Louisiana with French Settlers

in the 18th Century
I was even grown at Monticello
by Thomas Jefferson . . .

In another poem entitled "The Two Friendly Geese" she says,

We ruffle our feathers
and do the goose step
against our enemies
over skin color, hair color, and eye color
height and weight,
disabilities . . .

This particular poem is a history lesson in the American experience. Reed has done her homework on the historical origins of things and all throughout the book it becomes more and more apparent. Having a famous literary dad, Ishmael Reed; she certainly has benefited via osmosis and/or genes by being raised by a performing artist mother, Carla Blank; and a father who celebrates the WORD. Once, she points out in a poem that she was asked, "Who's the better writer?" She replied, "We write differently."

There are lines in Reed's poetry that are like sudden postcards that must be savored. In the poem "Jerusalem" it opens with:

It's a Saturday night/Standing on Mount of Olives in East Jerusalem/
you can view the Old City . . .

But even when Reed captures the topographical essence of a place, she also brings to it a sense of History as in the poem that addresses the French, "Why No Flowers for Africa?"

What are the French doing in independent Africa?
Looting minerals, food and art . . .

She continues:

> Why is a life in France
> worth more grief and anger
> than a life in Nigeria, Mali . . .

Back in America we get another atmospheric poem opening with lines on a visit to New Orleans:

> While horse drawn carriages await them/tourists meander
> down Decatur Street
> in the September heat . . .

These are the opening lines of a poem that explores a search to visit the city's famous "Congo Square" now called Louis Armstrong Park. Arriving she describes what they found:

> We see no mention on site that this is where
> Africans were routinely bought and sold . . .

Back on her own turf, Reed mourns a friend lost to violence and gunfire. Her poem "For Antonio Ramos" explains,

> I told you I was angry at the ICE agent
> who left his gun in plain view in his car
> so the young man who shot you
> was able to grab it when he broke into that agent's car
> That's how he robbed you of your camera
> at gunpoint
> when all you had was a paintbrush

Reed speaks about not only injustice across the pond in Europe and Africa but also the injustice which is right on her doorstep. In the poem "L.R. Californicus, Part II" she addresses the gentrification that has ethnically cleansed San Francisco but is threatening Oakland, California.

Most of the Blacks who
once occupied the area
are dead, priced out
or foreclosed to other cities . . .

She continues:

A woman with tattoos
up and down her arms
walks two more
tan and white pit bulls
Why so many pit bulls?
Are they four legged Zimmermans
Patrolling the Blacks who remain?

Tennessee Reed is a poet to watch, to savor, to support in her
witnessing of our time!

Ase!
Philadelphia, Pennsylvania 2019

*Califia Burning*
*New and Selected Poems,*
*1987-2019*

# The Mid-Afternoon Brain Freeze

It is a Tuesday afternoon in June of 2011
I go to the Starbucks at City Center Plaza in Oakland
where the former American, United and Delta ticket office
were turned into an AAA Insurance Office,
Top Dog, Wells Fargo, Dress Barn, Jamba Juice
and Panda Express

Down at the bottom is BART's 12th Street station
I go purchase a double espresso for Dad
It is 3:00 on the dot
There is a long line
even though it is a hot day
The line is filled with young people
dressed for work in suits, high heels or dress shoes
talking on their Bluetooth devices
to short stocky girls in their teens or early twenties
wearing short shorts, t-strap sandals and graphic tee shirts
with groups of three or four friends
There are a lot of people sitting alone at tables
reading books, working on laptops or tablets,
or listening to MP3 players
The place is packed with sounds
of customers having conversations,
the baristas shouting orders,
the machines filling up cups with coffee and whipped cream

and music blasting from the monitor to my right
describing the title, artist and album
I notice one young woman over by a window
working on her silver MacBook Pro
and sipping on an iced Mocha Frappuccino,
a mixture of espresso, sugar, cocoa, and low fat milk
inside of a clear plastic cup with the Starbucks logo on it
She sips it through a green straw

I finally get to the front and order one double espresso,
wait for it for five minutes,
and then head back
through the rotunda of the Federal Building
consisting of twin towers joined by a bridge
to relocated Victorian homes
turned into offices named Preservation Park
shaded by trees,
surrounded by a white picket fence with climbing roses
where people are gathered on the grass in front of a gazebo
to hand Dad his double espresso
He is sitting on a wrought iron bench
behind the Persian fountain
underneath an old fashioned street lamp
"There was a long line," I said
"Everyone was having their mid-afternoon brain freeze."

# A Sonnet to American Airlines

Our 737 could not fly
We were transferred to Gate H8
To prepare to board Flight 1835
We boarded over two hours late
The 738 was stuck in tow
The captain's sense of humor was dry
When we were to leave he did not know
Finally we took off into the sky
The flight attendant threw napkins at me
She didn't even look me in the eye
The girl in front of me rode on my knees
The plane bounced along the windy sky

The humming of the engines was quite loud
We descended through black, patchy clouds

# New York City Villanelle

They got off at what she called a dump
She said it's not too promising
He called them both a grump

They saw one cop fall on his rump
While onlookers gathered around the scene
They got off at what she called a dump

The continental breakfast was a sorry lump
Instant coffee, not coffee beans
He called them both a grump

The subway schedule had her stumped
To figure it out she had to be keen
They got off at what she called a dump

The Bed-Stuy avenue shops displayed finery and junk
Some of the items seemed obscene
He called them both a grump

At MoMA's Cindy Sherman show she was pumped
When it comes to photography she is a fiend
They got off at what she called a dump
He called them both a grump

# Lake Temescal Caste Royale

The hybrid mallards are large and the purebred mallards are small
Denizens of a landscape perfect as a Hudson River School
   keepsake
Except the hybrids swim miserably in a pond-like tight crawl
banned to a clogged culvert's severe algae outbreak
Allowing the purebreds to occupy the flowing comfort of
   Temescal's grand lake
if it is possible to exclude from vision the hybrids
huddled amidst the toxic, stagnant yellow liquid

# City Dwellers, Part Two

*(Sequel to City Dwellers)*

It is around 4:45 in the afternoon on August 24, 2012
I go outside to water the plants
I hear rustling sounds
in the angel's trumpet tree
At first I think it is a flock of birds
Then I think it is a cat so I make a catty sound
I see a tail flash by in the neighbor's yard
It is light brown with wide, dark brown stripes
"Oh, it is a raccoon," I say to myself
It is rare for them to be out in daylight

Around 6:30 pm I see three of them in our yard
I call them "Bandit," "Scavenger" and "Hisser"
It is still light out
They are eating lettuce that we are growing
I take tons of pictures of them
One keeps looking at the camera
with its beady, black eyes
through the brown-black mask on its face
that goes from its forehead to its nose
Another glances at the camera
It makes a low, long hiss
The third is too busy eating to notice me

They are not like forest raccoons
These are obese, city raccoons,
too well adapted to urban life
It sounds like an army
pounding up the back stairs
to our roof porch
where they have their
noisy evening parties
They leave their do on the porch
Our friend takes ammonia
and sprinkles it on the porch
to repel them
In two days they figured out
it would not be a problem for them
the same way they figured out one device
with a high pitched sound
that only animals can hear
including me
and another, the infrared light
promised to annoy them
by flashing in their eyes
We hire someone to trap them
before we go to Jerusalem
Instead they trap a skunk
I didn't even know skunks were in this area
"I paid $450 to trap a skunk," Dad says
A second skunk is trapped
while we are in Jerusalem
A friend informs me the whole house
smells of skunk
Later we discover
fresh red chili pepper powder will keep raccoons away

Right before we go on our trip
yellow jackets hang out
next to Mom's window

in the master bedroom
They have made a nest under the roof
We ask the person who we hired
to trap the raccoons to get rid of these wasps
The next morning the yellow jackets figure out
how to come into the house
through openings at the top of the back windows' hardware
Dad kills one after the other with rolled up magazines
by smashing them against the window
Later, one flies into the house and goes right for him
while he sits at the computer in the dining room
It stings him on the hand in retaliation
because it was Dad who killed its swarm mates
The exterminator apologizes
for forgetting to seal the holes
Dad's hand still feels that sting

In October of 2012
a camera crew arrives
to film Dad
They inform us that
there is a large spider
in the Meyer lemon tree
located in the front yard
I go outside to take photos
I call him King Kahuna
He is an orb weaver spider
He is a tan color
with wide, milk chocolate stripes
on his opisthosoma and prosoma
and narrow yellow and brown
stripes on his legs and palps
King Kahuna is eating a grasshopper
and his opisthosoma is swollen
from trying to consume the grasshopper
Orb weavers are commonly found in gardens

I see King Kahuna a few days after that
with a new web
He has eaten all of his
spiral-wheel webs
with their Velcro-like mechanism
to catch prey
each evening
One of his long legs keeps flickering
while watching a moth hanging
upside down in the web
As it gets colder
King Kahuna closes up shop

I make a joke with Mom
that everyone enjoys her plants
whether they have two legs,
four legs, six legs or eight legs

# The Two Friendly Geese

Behind the South Berkeley Post Office
a dozen generic domestic geese,
used as guard animals,
wander around a large yard
A farm goose,
possibly a hybrid of European,
African and Asian descent,
and an Embden goose,
whose ancestors are from the North Sea,
stretch their long necks upwards
as soon as they see me
They waddle in my direction
A white lattice fence separates us
The farm goose bends his neck towards me
and sniffs me with his black beak
He greets me with a loud honk
The Emden goose, who is all white,
also honks a greeting at me
The farm goose poses for a picture
by turning his head to the left,
and showing me his neck,
which is a mixture of light brown and white
The Emden goose continues to stare at me
with beady black eyes, and it smells me
with its orange beak

As I turn around to leave
I notice they are watching me
As I get in the car, they are walking back
towards their group

Unlike the geese
we are goosed
They are content
while we are grousing
The geese unite
not caring about where they came from
We can learn from them,
or are we far from learning
from those who are considered lower than we,
the prize of the universe?

Before our hiss takes the form
of nuclear warheads
and climate change
We ruffle our feathers
and do the goose step
against our enemies
over skin color, hair color, and eye color
height and weight,
disabilities,
ethnicity, nationality,
political
and religious beliefs,
land and property
We determine our standards upon
where people come from,
what they wear,
their education and profession,
how much money they make,
how old someone is,
what type of music they listen to,

what kinds of food they eat
who they choose to worship

While geese tolerate each other,
regardless of their roots,
harmony among humans
is still a wild goose chase

# Dear Grandma Reed

Dear Grandma Reed,

I can't believe it has almost been a year since you have passed on. That was fast. I think about you every day and I know that you are looking over me. The last time I spoke with you was over the phone right after Dad's birthday and right before mine. That was about a week and a half before your passing. A few hours after you passed, I heard you calling my name. On my flights to and from Buffalo, I saw your face in the clouds. You were smiling at me, which meant I knew you weren't suffering anymore.

I tucked a note with your name inside a crack in the Wailing Wall in Jerusalem to let you know I am thinking about you. Around Christmas of 2012 you came to me in a dream. You were saying in your melodious voice that you were "Haappy, haappy, haappy," and that you were preparing dinner for the Lord, Grandpa Bennie and Little Vincent. You were wearing your red sweater and black slacks. You had baked your famous brownies and a turkey and some corn bread was just about ready in the oven. You were relaxing with a bottle of beer. I woke up feeling happy.

When I look at the photos of you from over the years, I remember our visits. I remember our white Christmases in 1996 and 2003, us taking you to Hawaii in June of 1994, and my two week visit to Buffalo in June of 1988 right after fifth grade ended. That was when I really got to know you, Grandpa Bennie,

Uncle Bennie and Aunt Crystal, Uncle Vincent, Aunt Linda and my cousins Tasheka, Crystal, Bennie and Vincent. I remember going to the AME Zion Church with you, all dressed up just so. When I see you looking at me in the photos, I know you are still with me.

Love,
Tennessee

# Miami: A Mural

Miami sits
in the far southeast corner
of the United States
In the night
the reds, purples, and blues
of the city
sparkle on the black waters
of Biscayne Bay

The sun shines
over the downtown buildings
while rain clouds
part over Ocean Drive
and the beach
after a rapid deluge
The muggy air smells fresh
from the rains

Tourists have lunch
underneath the logo decorated awnings
of the colorful Art Deco hotels
including the Carlyle
designed in 1939
by Richard Kiehnel
and John Elliot

and renovated into
nineteen private luxury condos
with full kitchens,
Jacuzzi tub/showers,
washer/dryers
and cable
and high speed internet access
Several films,
including the 1996 film *The Birdcage*
with Robin Williams, were filmed there

Unlike the Bay Area
people come out
on a stormy Wednesday evening in September
to hear a poetry reading
at Books&Books
in the suburb of Coral Gables
You might even get Haitian writer
Edwidge Danticat to attend
Down the street
from the Mutiny Hotel
in the Coconut Grove neighborhood,
with two-bedroom suites
that look out over the Bay,
and an oval shaped swimming pool,
is a Gap,
a CVS Pharmacy
and a police horse
tied to a tree
despite the heat and humidity
A bit of the old South
plopped down
in the middle of a city
with the rhythm of the Marimba

On Collins Avenue
inside a small gym
people run on treadmills,
ride stationary bikes and use the stair master
The lights in the room
are pink and blue
like the American Airlines
737-800 with the
Boeing Sky Interior

In a South Beach
residential neighborhood
called Palm Island,
separated by the MacArthur Causeway,
a three-tiered flowing fountain surrounded
by Royal and Coconut palm trees
commands the centerpiece for large mansions
The 1996 film *Blood and Wine*
with Jennifer Lopez
includes a scene located there

In South Pointe Park
sits Smith & Wollensky Restaurant
where Gloria Esteban's husband, Emilio
hangs out with his friends
on a Wednesday afternoon
and where his large, black van is parked
Their restaurant, Bongos Cuban Café,
offers the most expensive rice and beans in the country

Older men
and their younger girlfriends dine
at Smith & Wollensky
on a Sunday evening
From the park you can see
ships filled with goods

sailing into the Government Cut Canal
that runs from the Atlantic Ocean
to the bay
and the busy downtown skyline
filled with new condos
lit up in blues, greens, and golden browns
like 900 Biscayne Bay
with a fish tank in the ceiling,
and balconies that overlook the bay
and the Viceroy Icon Brickell
supported by imitation Moai, the stone Easter Island statues
that our friend, a local, calls potato heads

After a Miami Heat basketball game
at the American Airlines Arena
thousands of fans fill the streets
excited from watching LeBron James, Dwayne Wade
and Chris Bosh do the Alley-oops, slam-dunks
and shoot three pointers brilliantly from the perimeters

On a quiet side street off of NE Second Avenue
between the Hilton Miami Downtown
and Miami Dade College Wolfson Campus
lay homeless people, mostly Black men,
sleeping in tents,
their carts filled with
recycled soda cans and bottles,
blankets, and second hand clothes

At Tap Tap Haitian Restaurant
on 5th Street in South Beach
murals cover the walls
There is one of Erzulie
the Haitian loa
of love, beauty, jewelry,
dancing, luxury and flowers

At the Hilton Miami Downtown
a noisy crowd of people fill the ballroom for a gala
The men come in black tie
The women wear ball gowns
or short cocktail dresses
One woman wears a long, purple gown
The top barely covers her large breasts
which look like they are about to pop out
Her arm is wrapped around her boyfriend's waist
A group of tall, thin girls get out of a stretch limo
wearing black dresses that barely cover their thighs
An older blonde woman gets off the elevator
with her husband
She has so much makeup on
she looks like the Bride of Chucky
She is wearing a backless
wine colored gown

In Miami
English is a Second Language
People say "Hòla"
instead of "Hello"

# Brussels Sprouts

I immigrated to the U.S.
from my birthplace,
Brussels, Belgium,
where I lived
since 1587
taking the long journey
to Louisiana with French Settlers
in the 18ᵗʰ Century
I was even grown at Monticello
by Thomas Jefferson

I moved to California in the early 1900s
I am mostly grown in the central coast region
where the cool climate reminds me of Belgium
I am shipped to Berkeley Bowl
where I am picked up by Carla
and taken to the Reed home
Roasted in olive oil at dinner time,
and dressed in lemon juice,
I am placed in front of Tennessee
on a cobalt blue plate
along with brown rice
and a chicken apple sausage

Tennessee picks me up
with a tiny fork
and I feel myself
being crushed by thirty-two teeth
and the gulping sound
as her epiglottis closes

# Dear P!nk:

Now that you're a wife and mother
you seem to have calmed down a lot
You even say you're only a "tad angry"
I wonder what lyrics come to your head
when you change diapers,
check to see if your daughter
has a temperature and a pulse
Or when you and your daughter dance
and go on bike rides
will you write songs about your family?

I must admit
it took me a while
to get into your music
But when I bought your album,
*M!ssundaztood* for my sister,
who is one of your biggest fans,
and she played it in her apartment,
I really began to enjoy your work
My favorite songs of yours are
"Just Like A Pill," "Stupid Girls,"
"So What," "Blow Me (One Last Kiss),"
"Try" and "Just Give Me A Reason"
I listen to these songs
when traveling and exercising

Just like you
had chronic asthma as a child
I had chronic ear infections
You began writing lyrics
as a teenager to express yourself
I was even younger when I started
writing poems to express myself
It seems like we both entered the public stage early
as I had books published
and you had albums come out
before we were considered adults

You travel the world
doing concert tours
I travel the world
doing poetry readings and workshops
Over the years your style of singing has changed
and my poetry keeps changing also

# Tanasi River

I was named after you
I saw the Tennessee River
652 miles
connecting from the Ohio River
through Tennessee and Alabama
to the Mississippi River
I crossed its bridges
in between Chattanooga and Hixson
and Florence and Muscle Shoals
It splits Chattanooga in two
like the Danube splits Buda and Pest

This river has had many names:
the River of the Cherokees,
the Caquinampo, Kasqui,
Hogohegee and Acanseapi
A Cherokee village once inhabited its banks

It served as routes
for explorers and fur traders,
the Confederacy,
and General Ulysses S. Grant's
Federal army

In 1933,
as part of the
Tennessee Valley Authority
under Franklin Roosevelt,
dams were built
for navigation,
power and flood control
like the Chickamauga Dam
in Chattanooga
named after a tribe
that broke away from the Cherokee
and lived near Chickamauga Creek

Its mussels fed the ancient Mound Builders
who crushed their shells to make their
pottery strong
The mussels are almost extinct
but people still dive in the river to catch them

Great Blue herons
stand on one leg along its banks
as they look out into the water
or walk along the rocks
even though the river is full of toxic metals,
antibiotics, antidepressants,
cholesterol lowering medications,
pesticides, fertilizers and coal fly ash
from the TVA Kingston Fossil Plant spill of 2008
when the slurry spilled into the Emory River
that flows into the Tennessee
damaging surrounding homes and land
The cleanup will take years

I watched two men
load their catch
of black basses

and black crappies
into the back
of their Ford pick-up truck
Pregnant women
and children
are told not to eat the fish
Everyone else,
only once a month
I wonder what the Cherokee would think

A sign warns people to move to higher ground
in cases of rapidly rising water
It reminded me of the Cherokee myth
"The Haunted Whirlpool"
about the "Suck Creek" or "Pot-on-the-water"
near Chattanooga
where canoe men
clung onto the bank
as the waters rose
Some were lucky
like one man who was
swept into a whirlpool
He was pushed into shallow waters
and climbed out onto the bank
Another went underwater
where, like is said of Atlantis,
a village of people
tried to draw him down into their home
He was pulled away to safety

I wonder what would happen
if the first natives were alive today
when an inch and a half of rain falls
in the area in an hour or two
and flood watches and tornadoes are more frequent
Will the Tennessee Valley eventually

repeat "The Deluge" of Chattanooga in 1867
when people, homes, farms, telegraph lines and bridges
drowned in the river?
It seems as if the Cherokee were predicting
the outcome of climate change

I was named after you

# Jerusalem

It's Saturday night
Standing on Mount of Olives in East Jerusalem
you can view the Old City
Hovering over other buildings to the west,
the eye is drawn to the Islamic shrine's golden sphere,
Dome of the Rock, which theoretically also sits
on the Temple Mount, said to be site of the Second Temple
making it the source of endless arguments both philosophical
and territorial
The Jordan River to the east
blends in with the clear sky
surrounding the city's lights flashing dots of red and yellow

In East Jerusalem, Palestinian neighborhoods'
hot, dry air stinks from trash long overdue for pick up
by the official Israeli collection agency
Stray cats roam around garbage:
Coca-Cola cans, diapers,
food scraps, wood,
and spoiled fruits and vegetables,
while Israelis enjoy fresh new high rise apartment buildings
near Hebrew University's Mount Scopus campus

Walking underneath the castle-shaped
Damascus Gate built during the Ottoman Empire

iPhone and iPad cases, printed fabrics, jelly shoes,
ice cream, water bottles and tee shirts saying,
"My grandmother went to Jerusalem
and all she brought was this lousy tee shirt,"
hang from the vaulted ceiling

The Western Wall Tunnels underneath the Old City
span from pre-Christian golden colored Western Stone
through ancient streets with Herodian columns
and the Struthion Pool or Water Channel
to modern day excavations intended to find remnants
of the First and Second Temples
Jewish women pray underground at the "Holiest of Holies,"
a wall beneath Temple Mount

The Western Wall or Wailing Wall
built by King Herod is packed
on a balmy Wednesday evening
between the High Holidays
Rosh Hashanah and Yom Kippur
Hasidic men in black hats and beards
watch to make sure
women obey their laws
and don't enter any prayer space
from which they are prohibited

At Garden Tomb
a Brazilian tour group
in uniformed black tee shirts
worships in Portuguese
singing hymns
Partially hidden behind trees
they are lined up in rows
in front of white painted wooden benches
A Brazilian flag
flies above them, hanging from a tree

opposite the rock "Golgotha,"
its "skull" believed to have been
scorched into a hillock
upon the death of Jesus
Inside the tomb a sign reads,
"He is not here for He has risen"

Walking down Via Dolorosa
Or "Way of Grief,"
satellite dishes
and solar panels
from the residential
neighborhoods above
make a circular pattern
Mini-marts, antique shops
and a computer repair shop
line up between the
Fifth Station of the Cross
and Lion's Gate
An American pastor
serving as a tour guide
leads two Americans
down the winding cobblestone street
Russian Orthodox
and Italian Catholic pilgrims
sing praises

On Lions' Gate Street
a woman dressed in all black
accented with a hot pink hijab
and matching hot pink handbag
strolls down the steep steps
toward the street's arched entrance
after stopping to speak with another woman
at an outdoor cafe

Further down
a little boy runs ahead of his mother
down an even steeper side street of stone stairs
from an apartment building at the top

In West Jerusalem at Malcha Mall,
on a late Friday morning,
before the city shuts down
for Jumu'ah Prayer and Shabbat,
people sprawl around the two story
contemporary outdoor scene sporting shopping bags
from American Eagle, Adidas, Toys "R" Us, Office Depot and Zara
before climbing the stairs to enter Jaffa Gate
above the highway tunnel
that heads towards
Tel Aviv/Ben Gurion International Airport

# L.R. Californicus

Part One

It is around 1:00 PM
on May 6, 2013
I, the Mearns bobcat sub-species
of California,
west of the Sierra Nevada,
am minding my business,
hunting in the tall grass
near the Marin Headlands Arts Center
for insects, rabbits,
small rodents and deer
It is unusual for me to hunt
at this time of day
I am supposed to be resting
in a thicket
I usually hunt the three hours
before sunset to midnight
and then before dawn
and the three hours after sunrise
My prey has different schedules
now that it is the driest year
on record

My keen sense of hearing
makes me hear a car door slam
I look up and with my sharp
sense of vision,
I see two women,
one younger
and one middle aged,
looking in my direction
The young woman is wearing
jeans and a tee shirt
and the middle-aged woman
a brown top, khakis and a hat
I hear, "What do you think that is?
Do you think it's a coyote
or a fox?" from the middle aged woman
The younger woman
zooms in her
Nikon Coolpix P90
I sit down
and turn my head to the left

My ancestors have been here
for 1.8,000,000 years
but the people think
they own the place
They build their homes
in the woods, mountains
and deserts where I
and my relatives live,
yet they want to kill me
because they think I am a threat
They dump their trash
as they take their hikes or camp
and they even mix us
with their domestic cats
to possess an "exotic" animal

I hear the younger woman
in an excited voice say,
"It's a cat. It's a bobcat."
My bright green eyes
blend in with the grass
My tawny face
with white muzzle
and white chin,
and a brown striped pattern
on my cheeks and forehead
poke out
The black tufts on my ears
stick up

After I pose for the photo
I go back to hunting
I hear the women get back in their car,
turn the motor on,
and take off
I feel more at ease


Part Two

I know how this bobcat feels
Our street and surrounding streets
have also been swept up
by an invasion of
predominately White techies, yuppies
and millennials from San Francisco
Most of the Blacks who
once occupied the area
are dead, priced out
or foreclosed
to other cities:
Antioch, Vallejo,
Stockton and Castro Valley

Since the UCSF Benioff Children's Hospital employees
started saving money by parking on our street
instead of their Rubik's Cube of a garage
and ever since the Bakery Lofts
were built down the street
where the Wonder Bread factory
sold day-old bargains
it is hard to park the car
in front of the house
On street sweeping days it is worse

When I back out of the driveway
it is more complicated
and dangerous
with the big, red whale of a car
or jumbo silver Dodge RAM
parked in front of our house
when there is plenty of space
across the street
in front of their house

In the pre-gentrification days
it was rude
not to acknowledge your neighbors
when meeting on the street
with at least a "good day" or "how are you?"
These days, hardly any of the newcomers
even so much as nod at us as they pass by
and sadly, I've taken to that style as well
except for those we have really come to know

A young couple
walks their
tan and white pit bull
while they push their infant
in a jogging stroller

A woman with tattoos
up and down her arms
walks two more
tan and white pit bulls,
one leash in each hand
Why so many pit bulls?
Are they four legged Zimmermans
patrolling the Blacks who remain?
An older, gray haired couple
walk their two English collies each morning
They look like real live Lassies
They let their dogs
do their do on our lawn
They don't pick it up

Our next door neighbors
ask in a panic,
"Do you know if our neighbors
have a beehive?
There is a swarm in our backyard,
and they look like
they are coming into yours."
A cloud of bees hover around
the rosemary bushes
The beekeeper
comes to the front door
suited up and says,
"I have come to collect my bees."
A few months later her housemate
pounds on the front door
His drone got stuck in the camellia bush
He offers a jar of honey from the bees
I use some in my tea
It tastes better than store bought honey

As someone said,
"As soon as you get rid of one pest,
another one comes along."
These particular pests ride bicycles

# Swimming

Swimming can be like writing
It can be quick and short
or slow and long

Starting a poem can be hard
like diving into cold water
from a racing block

It can be like the IM (Individual Medley)
where a lot of thoughts can be
spilled out into one stanza
like when one does the freestyle,
backstroke, breaststroke and butterfly
all within one hundred yards

Sometimes writing a poem
takes a while to get perfect
like the breast stroke:
glide, kick, breathe
or it just comes out
like the 50 yard 50
Sometimes the pace of ideas
continues like with flip turns
during a 400 meter freestyle

Different poems
are like the different
speed lanes
in an Olympic swimming pool:
slow, medium and fast

Ending a poem can be intense
like climbing out of the
toasty, steaming water
of the Spieker Aquatic Complex
pool at Cal
on a cold, rainy, February day

# How High the Moon

Did you see the pink Strawberry
Super Moon in June
or the orange September Harvest moon
rising over the Oakland Hills
on a fogless night?
What about the August Sturgeon Moon
that looked blue?
The moon is 4.5 billion
year old debris
after impact
between Earth and Mars
The Apollo 11
landed there in 1968
I wonder what the view
of the Earth looked like
238,900 miles (or one light year away),
its crust, mantle and core
changing colors each month
From earth I can see its "maria"
or lunar plains
and some of its 300,000 craters
when I zoom in with my
Nikon Coolpix P510

There was a face on the
crescent moon in October
It was looking down at me
at the DoubleTree by Hilton Hotel
Berkeley Marina
before the fog rolled in
Maybe it was Chang'e,
the Chinese immortal moon goddess,
who swallowed the pill of immortality
Her husband, Houyi
sought the Queen Mother of the West
to ban the mortality punishment
cursed on him by the Jade Emperor
for killing his nine sons
Chang'e rose up into the heavens
until she landed on the moon

The Full Hunter's Moon of October
invokes the Greek goddesses:
Selene, goddess of the moon
and the goddess of the hunt,
Artemis of Mount Latmos
They remind us that they resurrected
the island of Patmos
after it had sunken into the sea

In December
Iemanjá, the Yoruba moon goddess
of the ocean, motherhood and children
rises during dusk over the pine trees
at the Strawberry Canyon Fire Trail
in the hills above UC Berkeley
before she reaches her fullest point
Venus sets to the west
and Jupiter rises to the east
A few days later

Iemanjá is dressed
in her fine, evening gown
of turquoise, orange and black
In Brazil, people dress in white
and flock to Copacabana Beach
in Rio de Janeiro
to offer her jewelry, perfume,
combs, lipstick, white flowers
and mirrors

On the 2nd of January
the new Wolf moon shines
against the purple dusk sky
As it begins to wane on January 23rd
it makes a silver half circle
in the morning sky

The February Snow Moon
is my favorite
At sunset it rises
gleaming in white and pink
In the darkness it peeks through
the black clouds
shining gold
By the time my birthday comes around
it has completely waned

As Daylight Savings Time
arrives in March
the Crow Moon
lingers over downtown Berkeley
at 4:15 in the afternoon
signaling the end of winter is near
and the crows will make
their last caws of the season

When the moon hits your eye
like a big pizza pie
that's amore
I'll take the moon any way
it presents itself to me
whether it's only a paper moon
the moon river
the old devil moon
the shine on harvest moon
the moon over Miami
the blue moon
many moons ago
or Joy Harjo's
moon as in
"What moon drove me to this?"

Moon, what would we do
without you
The star that spices up
the sky

# Strawberry

Not many people know
that I am a mixture
of French, American and Chilean

I get around the world
At Wimbledon
they have a tradition
to dump cream on top of me
In Sweden I am a treat
on Midsummer's Eve
In Greece
I am sprinkled with sugar
and dipped in Metaxa
In Italy I make a
special tiramisu

I contain the most
antioxidants
of all of the fruits
I help with diabetic
kidney failure,
Alzheimer's disease,
and heart disease

The Algonquin Tribe
named the June moon
after me
That is my harvesting season

There is even
a Strawberry Canyon
above UC Berkeley
where people go for a swim
and take a hike

Even though I am attacked
by moths, fruit flies, aphids,
mold and mildew,
By late Spring or early Summer
I still arrive
in dessert bowls

# I've Got the Climate Change Blues

There's a drought in California
and record snowfall in the East
I say there's a drought in California
and record snowfalls in the East
We have to ration water
and pay more money for what we eat

Washington State had mudslides
and Dallas had a major snowstorm
Washington State had mudslides
and Dallas had a major snowstorm
Thousands of flights were cancelled
and Super Typhoon Haiyan took form

There's a drought in California
and record snowfalls in the East
Here it feels like summer in winter
and we pay more for what we eat

The hay fever started early
when cherry blossoms began to bloom
The hay fever started early
when cherry blossoms began to bloom
The dog shed her winter coat in January
Smoggy air loomed and loomed

There's a drought in California
and record snowfalls in the East
We have to ration water
and pay more for what we eat

There's a shortage of tornadoes
and an active hurricane season
There's a shortage of tornadoes
and an active hurricane season
Even while in drought,
hail and thunderstorms are more common
throughout the Bay Area region

There's a drought in California
and record snowfalls in the East
Here it feels like summer in winter
and we pay more money for what we eat

The bears came out of hibernation in February
and mosquitoes bit me on a hot April afternoon
The bears came out of hibernation in February
and mosquitoes bit me on a hot April afternoon
The boars were roaming San Ramon
and Chinook salmon spawning ended too soon

There's a drought in California
and record snowfalls in the East
We have to ration water
and pay more for what we eat

# The Ethnic Blues

They like *Dances with Wolves*
and *Gone with the Wind*
They like *Dances with Wolves*
and *Gone with the Wind*
They feel these movies are romantic
With their racism they are determined

He doesn't support "political correctness"
and says the NAACP is a joke
He doesn't support "political correctness"
and says the NAACP is a joke
Without them he would never have gotten his pilot's license
Maybe he got this opinion from his folks

They like *Pocahontas*
and *Gone with the Wind*
They think these movies are metaphorical
With their racism they are determined

At their house parties

their guests look and think like they
At their house parties
their guests look and think like they
They live in the hills and suburbs
They don't give outsiders the time of day

They like *Django Unchained*
and *Gone with the Wind*
They assume these movies are accurate
With their racism they are determined

They support Hillary Clinton
and praise Barbara Bush
They support Hillary Clinton
and praise Barbara Bush
They like to insult Obama
At gatherings this is their ambush

They like *Birth of a Nation*
and *Gone with the Wind*
They claim these movies are historical
With their racism they are determined

They make jokes about ethnic names
of Whites, Asians, Blacks and Jews
They make jokes about ethnic names
of Whites, Asians, Blacks and Jews
They say their holocaust is the worst holocaust
Their ignorant jesting continues

They like *Peter Pan*
besides *Gone with the Wind*
They consider these movies funny
With their racism they are determined

They voted Green Party slate
and praised Cornel West
They voted Green Party slate
and praised Cornel West
He told Black people
not to vote for Hillary
He said Bernie was best

They like *Mulan*
besides *Gone with the Wind*
They believe these movies are rhetorical
With their racism they are determined

Their ancestors might have had
Thanksgiving with the Pilgrims
or told fellow slaves
not to run away
Their ancestors might have had
Thanksgiving with the Pilgrims
or told fellow slaves
not to run away
Maybe they were melting pot Jews
who ate pork during the holidays

They like *Temple of Doom*
and the all-time box office favorite *Gone with the Wind*
They find these movies allegorical
With their racism they reap the whirlwind

# Hapalochlaena Lunulata

On *World's Deadliest Animals Australia*
a young man is hiking along the rocks
with his girlfriend
on the continent's south coast
He has shoulder length hair
and wears a gray tee shirt,
a black vest, long khaki shorts with a belt
and black Birkenstock sandals
It is daytime
He notices the Blue Ringed Octopus
resting in a tidal pool,
its yellow shape covered with dark brown rings

As he reaches down
into the pool
The octopus's rings expand,
darkening into a peacock blue
They pulse a warning

The young man
ignores the clue
He gets bitten
when he picks up the octopus
Through the octopus's beak
venomous tetrodotoxin enters the young man's body

He lies shaking on the beach
eyes dilated in respiratory arrest

There is no antidote
for this golf-ball sized cephalopod's bite
as humans rarely interact with it
Heart massage
and artificial respiration
are the only methods
to withdraw the toxin

As the paramedics arrive
the octopus swims away,
its blue rings fading back to brown

A moral is supposed to go here
but it is unnecessary

# Spike the Iguana

It is a Saturday afternoon at Lake Merritt
I am visiting the Rotary Nature Center by the aviary
where I study the dioramas,
Glass-cased taxidermy,
of many Pacific shorebirds,
the American black bear,
and the mountain lion
I observe an active honeybee hive,
the tarantula with its waiting cricket meal
and the California tuxedo king snake
who's curled up asleep, as always
There is a cage with two abandoned mallard ducks
who will live in the lake by the Dunsmuir House
once their feathers return

I exit the nature center
and see a young woman taking pictures
I walk over to see what interests her
As I get closer
I realize the photographer
is an elementary school friend
photographing an iguana
sunning itself in the potted plants
It looks up at me
and watches me walk towards it
its dewlap extended under its jawbone

It's a myth that this always means it's threatened
It may have been saying hello
or just trying to find
a comfortable body temperature

I get out my phone to take photos
It sticks its tongue out to smell me
and my phone
From one of the nature center's staff members
I find out its name is Spike
and that it is a female
She is thirteen years old
and previously someone's pet
He says I can touch her
because I'm curious
about how her skin feels
She feels like a ton of needles
She closes her eyes and relaxes
I pet her spine,
which looks like a dorsal fin
and unlike humans, is outside her body

When I take pictures of her
She looks right into the camera
A crowd of people surround her
taking photos
She looks around at everyone
and into the various cameras
A little girl keeps saying, "She's amazing."
A guy asks if that was the kind of animal
that attacked Sharon Stone's husband
The nature center's staff member comes out
and puts lettuce in front of her
She begins to eat
When I say goodbye
she watches me go

# Family Feud

It has been a long July
A Palestinian American visits his cousin
for the first time since he was a small child
Following the kidnapping and death of three Israeli teenagers
his cousin is burned to death in East Jerusalem
The young American boy is beaten
and arrested by Israeli police
My East Jerusalem based friends
are scared to leave their homes
They get bombed shopping at the market

The cities in Gaza have been destroyed
as though they might have been hit by
an earthquake, tornado or hurricane
rather than bombs
A large, black cloud
billows from the rubble
A few beige skyscrapers
still stand in the distance

A father weeps over his dead child
One half of his child's head remains
Palestinians are all cried out
At the hospitals
their family, friends and neighbors

are wrapped in bandages like mummies,
most have shrapnel wounds treated,
others are missing arms and legs
as they lay in shock
A child remains motionless
with shrapnel in her spine and neck
Her mother and sisters are dead
Their home is destroyed
A bomb goes off next to the hospital

A University of Washington-bound woman
is unable to leave to start the fall semester
Eid goes uncelebrated
Nine children are killed on a refugee playground
A U.N. school is attacked six times
Diabetics are not able to get their dialysis
People bleed to death in their homes
Medics sit on the ground exhausted
A few of them weep
The emergency ward is overwhelmed
A family seeking shelter at the U.N. school
waits to send their sick kids to the hospital
because of the crowds of wounded civilians
Reporters wear bulletproof vests saying, "Press"
A pro-Israeli journalist insists
to have a bodyguard with him at all times
U.N. spokesman Chris Gunness breaks down on TV
after its school is bombed on Wednesday
Its Rights chief says Israel is going against international law
Israelis charge Palestine with genocide

Leaflets fall from the sky warning Gazans to leave their homes
I think of my friends over there
wondering whether they are safe
They say they have no water
now that Israel bombed Gaza's lone power plant

They hear three booms in one minute
"Imagine hearing that for twenty-four hours straight,"
one tells me
They would like to write their stories in a blog
but there's no electricity
This is what their day-to-day life is like,
feeling trapped with no escape
probably not sleeping as they worry about being bombed
Most of those who are wounded are civilians
They are not pro-Hamas, pro-Fata or pro-Israeli
They are living their everyday lives
at home with women, children and old people
in an overcrowded twenty-five mile strip of land
occupied by Turkey, Great Britain,
Egypt and Israel before this era of Hamas
Bibi says he wants to complete
the military defensive
and sends Israeli troops
to destroy the Hamas tunnels
The U.S. sends money and weapons
to support the Israelis
The massacre spills into August
There is no end in sight

They say Israel is the only place
for Jews to seek refuge
Some claim that
Palestinians have more options
of places to go than Israeli Jews
but when asked where Palestinians could go,
they have no answer
Some compare the murder of Israelis
to the massacre of Palestinians
but numbers show no comparison
Some say that Arabs hate Jews
but Jews don't hate Arabs

Hamas points the finger at Israel
and Israel points the finger at Hamas
while the Israeli parliament approves more settlements
in the occupied West Bank

People in Tel Aviv enjoy the beach
Palestinian children get killed on the beach
Some say Israel has the right to defend itself
What about the Palestinians
who are scared of being bombed
while going to the market or to the mosque
or after taking refuge in the U.N. safe area?
They have no power compared to the Israeli army
My Palestinian friends tell me that the media is biased
People on the left and right blame Obama
but this began before he was born
Some say Israel wants all of Palestine
others say Palestine wants all of Israel
Some say Israel has a right to exist
Palestine also has a right to exist
Some say they should coexist
Somewhere, Abraham and Ishmael are crying

# Like An Old Friend Whom You Had Given Up For Dead Rain Returns to Oakland

The sun rises over the Oakland hills
The sky is hues of pink, yellow,
orange, gold and blue
Scattered clouds linger from storms
The Blues Note Bird sings his song
"C, C, A flat"
His voice stands out
amongst the other chirping birds
Crows call from telephone wires
and from trees on the adjacent street
Canadian geese honk
as they fly over the house
towards Lake Merritt
People honk their horns as if to answer

Neighbors rush out of their houses
for work and school
They climb into cars and on buses
and squeeze onto BART
The noises of cars, buses and BART
on Market Street and MLK
can be heard from my bedroom window
Garbage trucks shake the house each Thursday
before the sun comes up

The neighbors' Border Collie/Australian Shepherd mix barks
as the dog walker picks her up
Fat calico cats and black cats
guard leftover Halloween pumpkins
on the porch of the duplex across the street
GQ the tuxedo cat and Frances the tabby cat
show up for their photography sessions
in their favorite spot on the stone steps
underneath the apple tree

The wind howls, whistles and shakes windows
the oak trees dance,
and chimes jingle
as the next rainstorm approaches
Due to the winds
unlike their usual flight pattern
planes fly over the house
as they come in from the northeast
They fly southwest and then turn west
to land at SFO

Plants perk up
welcoming the rain
The northern mockingbird
takes a bath shaking his feathers
in the bare ginkgo tree
The brown world becomes green again

# A Flat Will Survive the Sun

The key of A flat
reminds me of sunset
and the color gold
"Blues in A Flat"
"Maple Leaf Rag" by Scott Joplin
"Word to the Mutha!" by Bell Biv DeVoe
"What About Us" by P!nk
"Perfect" by Ed Sheeran
"One Last Time" by Ariana Grande
and "Rubber Band Clown"
by Twilight 22

The Solstice sunset
at Emeryville Marina
includes a jet stream
and two puffy clouds
lingering over the bay
Gold reflects
on the blue gray waters
as the sun goes down
over San Francisco

Seen from up at Golden Bear
a single cloud hovers
over Treasure Island

The sun is a bright white circle
with yellow and pink outlines
to the southwest of the island

Flying home from Miami
on American Airlines Flight #275
a low front approaches the area
shortly after take off
Streaks of hot pink
are sandwiched
within dark blue clouds
Later on
from my window
oranges and yellows appear
As the sky transitions
from indigo to black
the bright pinks and peaches
of the sun
form a firework

In five billion years,
as this middle aged star changes,
it will become a swollen red giant
sucking up Mercury, Venus, Earth and Mars
Exploding, it will become a white dwarf
and then a black dwarf
the size of earth
but a million times heavier and denser

But the key of A flat will still be here
with the sounds of comets,
black holes,
meteorites,
stars being born,
Saturn's rings,
Io, Europa, Calisto

and Ganymede,
the former planet of Pluto,
Wormholes,
and space debris

A flat will survive our sun

# Garden Duchess and Duke

On November 15, 2014
the female Anna's Hummingbird,
named after Anna Massena,
Duchess of Rivoli, and wife of
Duke François Victor Massena,
of Rivoli, an ornithologist,
pollenates the Bird of Paradise

Common to yards
and residential neighborhoods
of the Pacific coast
and the Southwest,
she hovers over the plant
looking for flying insects and nectar
after flying in
over the wooden gate
from another garden further south
in Oakland

This medium sized, stocky bird's
spotted brown body
emerald back,
dark pink throat,
and straight black bill
are in focus
while her wings are in motion blur

She only stays for a second
and then shakes off pollen
and dirt from her feathers
at the rate of 55 bps
before flying north
towards 54th Street
landing on a grand old tree
grown higher than the telephone wires
She rests before the beginning of mating
season in December
waiting for the buzzy song
from a red crowned male
when he makes a steep dive
ending with a pop

# Untitled in Two Parts

Part One

I don't care
I am the honey badger
of the Kalahari Desert
I am known as a snake killer
of the two most lethal snakes
on the African continent:
the puff adder
and black mamba
I paw at the puff adder
and chase the black mamba
up a tree
They can kill a man
in less than a day
with their dendrotoxin
and their cytotoxin
but I only go unconscious
for two hours
then wake up
and tear their flesh
with my sharp toes

Part Two

The humans
are a lot like me
They evolved from four legs
to two legs
while I developed
thick fur
to protect myself
against the thousands
of honey bee stings
as they catch me
sneaking off
with their precious nectar
like an insider trader
making off with stock market tips
Unlike these so-called civilized apes
I don't need utensils
to eat my dinner

# Sauced English Teacher

She always entered
the American literature course
walking fast in pointy toed high heels
An Anglophile,
she wore gray dresses with lacy collars
her long platinum hair
pulled up with two barrettes
at both temples
and she clutched
a black Coach valise

Smelling of Jack Daniel's
covered by a mixture of rose, apple
and cedar wood perfume,
the English teacher arrived one day
crying because two girls teased her
in her previous class on British Literature
They'd said she had "a pig face"

The high school
juniors and seniors
sat in a semi-circle
their binders and American literature textbooks opened
She quickly turned,
slamming the door shut

abandoning the class
to finish crying in private
There was no reaction from the students

When she returned
a senior said,
as she passed around a photo
of herself at the Tower of London,
"That's you? I thought it was a dog."
A junior said, "Oooooh ho ho.
Oh, that's cold."
"I'm going to get back at you
for what you said,"
the English teacher retaliated

Then she started the lesson
by announcing, "I don't want to teach
any writings by Blacks and Jews.
I don't want to be politically correct.
I'm sorry if that offends anyone."
A senior with impulse control problems replied,
"Yeah, PC, it's BS."
The room's ambient tones filled the silence
as the others sat there disappointed
not knowing what to say
For another senior who was always bored,
staring at a map of France tacked to the wall
and a poster of Versailles' main palace
hung next to the door
would serve as inspiration to visit Versailles and Paris
twenty years later
Finally, that senior asked if they could read literature
by Native American writers
To "accommodate" this request
she assigned Christopher Columbus' journals

She stayed for five more years
after that class graduated
One minute she was calling her students "devils,"
the next she was writing "I love you"
on their evaluations
She passed out drunk
during class one day
and wound up in the hospital
After multiple nervous breakdowns
finally she was sacked,
divorced her Episcopal reverend husband
and moved away
to live with her sister
She was never heard from again

# Earth's Black Hole

I am the sinkhole

I occur all over the world
I swallow a South Korean couple
walking down the street
They survive
unlike the five year old boy
swimming in an Oklahoma lake
who drowns
A relative who dived in to save him
drowns too
Trees mysteriously disappear
in a Louisiana bayou
I eat the 40th Anniversary
Chevy Corvette
at a museum
in Bowling Green, Kentucky
Intersections bend inward
in Guatemala City
after Tropical Storm Agatha
slams this city
built on volcanic deposits
In Sinkhole Alley,
named after me,
a man falls to his death

in his bedroom
and houses collapse
because of limestone caves
and farmers pumping underground
water for their crops

After five weeks of relentless rain
I open up in San Francisco's
Richmond District
exposing aged pipes
When the sand is washed away
and the road's weight
is no longer supported
water gushes from beneath me
I keep getting bigger
until crews decide to pour sand
into me with a steam shovel
and lay asphalt on top of the sand
Meanwhile, the neighborhood has no water
People stare at me
surrounded by yellow caution tape
as they walk their children to school
and they drive past me
in a roundabout way

In Sanica, Bosnia-Herzegovina
I create a crater
full of mud and debris
after sucking up
a full pond of water, its fish and surrounding trees
A local opined:
"All sorts of miracles happen
before the doomsday"

I don't always have to be ugly
In Wallace County, Kansas, tourists flock to see me
Children hike down to my 90 foot bottom
I am compared to the Grand Canyon
In Belize I am
the four hundred foot deep
Great Blue Hole
barrier reef
and at the Bimmah sinkhole in Oman
believed to have been created by a meteorite, Hawiyat Najm,"
which means "The Falling Star" in Arabic
I am also the Dahab Blue Hole
off the Sinai Peninsula in Egypt
where a Bedouin Legend
tells of a young woman who drowned in the hole
to escape the marriage her father had arranged
and who continues to lure young men
into her depths
when, swimming towards her arch
they become disoriented from lack of oxygen
and fall 328 feet to their deaths
On a rock near the Red Sea are their tombs
One filmed his death
It went viral on YouTube

I am earth's black hole

# Point of View of a Blood Orange

"Why is this orange a funny color?" she asked
as I sat in the chipped black ceramic bowl
chopped into pieces shaped like a kidney
amongst the strawberries, raspberries, blueberries
and mango
My vivid reds, blues and purples
that look like blood vessels
come from antioxidants

"It's a blood orange,"
was the reply I heard
in the distance
"Oh, I thought there was something
wrong with the orange,"
she said

Little does she know
I have been used for
upside-down cake,
marmalade,
Sicilian winter salad
with sliced fennel bulb and olive oil,
I am also a flavor for
gelato, sorbet, Italian soda,
and chocolate cake with coffee

My taste is both sweet and sour
depending on whether I am the Tarocco of Italy,
the Moro of Sicily or the Sanguinello of Spain
I even make a mean martini

I prevent and kill cancer cells,
lower blood pressure,
prevent heart disease and stroke
and ward off cataracts
I am full of Vitamins A and C

She enjoys eating me so much
that she made a poem out of me

# Children's Bizarre

At the Sheraton Grand Hotel in Sacramento
a cheerleading competition is going on
The girls walk around the lobby
in white and orange long-sleeved tops
with blue stripes on the arms and shoulders
Their short shorts are white with orange trim
They wear white socks and white Keds sneakers

In the public bathrooms the mothers chat
while they make up their daughters' faces
in front of three large mirrors
One girl around the age of eleven
has her head tilted
to allow her mother to apply eyeliner
Blue eye shadow sparkles in the bathroom light
"My husband doesn't like my putting false eyelashes
and eye shadow on my daughter
but it's part of the competition."
From the way she applies her own mascara,
the mother looks like she has llama lashes
A young woman of thirty-eight walks by
and shakes her head at the mothers

Walking down J Street to Starbucks
Eight-year-old girls practice
kneeling on their right knees
and waving their arms in the shape of a Y
They wear purple and white polyester blended fabric
pleated skirts with matching liners
Their faces shimmer with purple powder

At Starbucks, a six- or seven-year-old girl
sits cross-legged in front of a Princess Elsa back-pack
from the Disney movie *Frozen*
Her mother combs her hair
kneeling behind the back-pack
"Ow," the little girl keeps saying
Her mother clips the large,
orange bow in her daughter's hair
She's wearing smoky eye makeup
and a slicked back tight bun
She looks like a daytime raccoon
People in line stare at them
One gentleman whispers to his
conference group,
"These women dress their daughters up
like hookers. Did a pornography director
invent this style?"
A young man from the group
looks at the mother and daughter
and laughs
Another little girl about the age
of ten walks towards her friends
The leotard underneath her skirt
exposes the cheeks of her butt

I didn't hang around
to find out who won

# The Avalanche of Sils im Engadin

I am the Avalanche
I catch people by surprise
The morning sky reflects on the snow
giving it a blue tint
fooling tourists
into thinking it's a beautiful day
but half an hour later it begins to snow
causing me to still flow dangerously close
to the roads and villages below
From the distance you can see
that mountains are marked
with lines to warn people that I am here
Power poles are braced for my arrival
Black and yellow poles stick out of the snow
so people know how to stay on the roads
when the snow gets deeper

People walking Lake Sils
hear loud explosions in the distance
as I get bombed from helicopters
to prevent greater danger
and to force the flow to dissipate rapidly
after a late March/early April snow storm
at the 5,915 foot high Swiss resort area

The tourists begin to leave
the Upper Engadin
after spending Easter break
riding in horse drawn carriages
during snow flurries
up the hill towards the Hotel Waldhaus
to have pizza topped with ham,
taking ski lifts up to 10,000 feet,
driving down into the valley
to visit the medieval town of Soglio,
and shopping at Jimmy Choo's in Saint Moritz

A couple, fat and rich
who could have been
painted by George Grosz,
enter the Waldhaus restaurant
with a large black lab and a sheep dog
The wife, her face pumpkin orange
from a fake tan,
wears a black wig,
an ankle length mink coat,
and a gold linked choker,
so massive,
she cannot lower her chin
The skiers board buses in their gear
of helmets, ski suits, boots and poles
not knowing that their sport
can cause me to flow
I take them with me
burying them alive
until red helicopters come to rescue them
From experience
I'm sure that I'll have
my shot at them again

Every year some people never make it out

# Paris

The City of Lights
is not what it looks like
in TV shows and movies
like the Citi AAdvantage
credit card commercial,
Gilmore Girls
and Keeping Up with the Kardashians
where guests stay in fancy hotel rooms
with white silk sheets and piles of pillows
resting on king-sized beds
and French casement doors opening up
to wrought iron balconies
with a view of the Eiffel Tower
or the Seine and Notre Dame Cathedral
in the distance

Paris looks more like
Jerusalem with hilly side streets,
Washington, D.C. and Philadelphia
with row houses
and New York's Washington Square Park
with the Arc de Triomphe

During the Solar Eclipse
on March 20, 2015

crowds from all over the world
walk to the Palace of Versailles
after taking the RER-C train from Paris
We couldn't see the eclipse
because fog or smog obscured it
But three hundred and fifty-seven mirrors
lining one side of the Hall of Mirrors
reflected the view from arched windows
facing the gardens
where Neptune and mermaids
cavort in the pools of fountains
The Galerie echoes
with sounds of Japanese, Chinese,
Italian, German, Spanish, French and English
in this chamber where the
Treaty of Versailles was signed
Was the resulting chaos prophesized in the ceiling's
grandiose Charles Le Brun paintings
flaunting France's victories?

Our tour guide with his George Washington hairdo
proudly displays Marie Antoinette's bedroom
with its Boucher painting
and a plethora of flower patterns
suffocating the wall panels, chairs,
bedspread, pillows, and canopy
A tourist remarks to his family,
"With this kind of wallpaper,
she deserved to be beheaded."
I wonder if she had nightmares
of flowers attacking her?

Boulevard St. Michel in the Latin Quarter
is filled with Sorbonne students
going to buy books at Shakespeare & Co.
for their poetry classes

or walking to Starbucks
for café (a.k.a. Espresso)
or eating pizza at Del Arte
on a cold first day of spring evening

Early morning at the Louvre
people already stand in line
outside of the glass I.M. Pei pyramids
to purchase tickets
They ride down the escalator
heading towards the Roman section
They stop to snap photos
of the headless Winged Victory of Samothrace
continuing through exhibit rooms
crowned with lavishly Rococo painted ceilings
on their way to see the star attraction, Mona Lisa
where a shoving match of Cannon Mark III 5D cameras
and iPhone 6 pluses on selfie sticks
will allow their owners
bragging rights to their Facebook, Twitter and Instagram friends
that they were in the presence
of Lisa Gherardini, wife of Leonardo di Vinci
Barely anyone wanders through
the Near Eastern Antiquities
with its elegant profusion
of glazed Iranian jars and hand-woven Indian carpets
except for a middle school group
assigned to a field trip

Henry the IV's Place Royale,
renamed Place des Vosges by Napoleon in 1800,
forms a symmetrical square of thirty-six
French Renaissance homes
rising above a vaulted brick arcade
It gives respite from the crowds around more famous tourist haunts
On Sunday morning parents watch their kids play in the

park-like square
and pigeons coo as they hunt for crumbs along gravel footpaths
In No. 6, Victor Hugo's home,
a view of vermillion buds begin to peek
from branches of Linden trees
as seen from multi-paned windows of its murky dining room
furnished with a dark ebony wood table, chairs and cabinets
surrounded by deep green and soft pink flowered wallpaper

Champs-Elysées
gives a different scene
Eurasian magpies fly over
crowds walking Europe's grandest boulevard
where London Plane trees line up in rows
in front of Gap, H&M, Cartier,
Sephora, Hugo Boss and Christian Louboutin
The Arc de Triomphe
stands over a 12 street roundabout at its west end
Sightseers climb up 284 steps
to take skyline panoramic shots
with Samsung Galaxy phones
In the Restaurant Publicis Drugstore
families eat large cheddar cheeseburgers
with Sprite and fries

At the Eiffel Tower
people photograph themselves
framed within iron lattice girders
At the base, Magnolia tree buds bloom lavender flowers
Seine River cruises float by
where visitors can catch
different angles of the iconic design
built as centerpiece for the 1889 World's Fair
which remained the tallest
man-made structure in the world until
New York's Chrysler Building rose to that honor in 1930

The new moon rises
and Venus is a sparkling
white dot in the sky
as the sun sets over the Latin Quarter
where locals and foreigners
sit outside Starbuck's
having mint tea and butterfly cookies
A great way to end a Parisian vacation

# Why No Flowers For Africa?

Parisians, Syrians, Lebanese, Kenyans,
Nigerians, Malians, Indonesians and the Burkinabé
all suffer the consequences of war and fundamentalism
They sit at cafes, attend concerts and soccer matches,
go to school, stay in hotels, trying to escape for a better life
They see family and friends being killed

Parisians and tourists
are told to stay indoors
They can't live their everyday lives
We are asked to sympathize with them
because they can't see the Mona Lisa at the Louvre,
sip espresso at Les Deux Magots,
load up on baguettes on the Champs-Elysées
feel safe riding the Métro
and take in views from top of the Eiffel Tower
Their children are caught in the middle of a fight
they did not cause
The sins of colonialism
visited upon its children out to hear music
What are the French doing in independent Africa?
Looting minerals, food and art

The Eiffel Tower may be lit in the colors
of the Malian flag

but the Police Nationale
surround African immigrants
selling tiny knickknacks to tourists
at that same Eiffel Tower
and the National Gendarmerie
send them
to Charles de Gaulle Airport
where they are kicked
out of "the city of lights"

All we hear about on the news are the attacks in Paris
Why don't we hear as much about attacks in Syria, Nigeria,
Kenya, Mali, Lebanon, Indonesia, and Burkina Faso?
Beirut got attacked the day before Paris,
Nairobi seven months before,
and Nigeria, Mali, Indonesia and Burkina Faso afterwards
What about ISIS raping women and children in their camps
or Boko Haram kidnapping two hundred Nigerian girls and
killing thirty people in a suicide bombing?

People said, "Je suis Paris"
and "Prayers for Paris"
but no "I am Beirut,"
"I am Bamako,"
"I am Nairobi,"
"I am Jakarta,"
and "I am Ouagadougou"

They made the French flag
their profile picture on Facebook
but where are the sightings
of the Nigerian, Malian, Kenyan,
Syrian, Lebanese, Indonesian
or Burkinabé flags

On the news we watched
a drowned Syrian child
washed ashore near the Turkish resort of Bodrum
or families walking hundreds of miles to Hungary
to catch a train to Austria or Germany
only to be turned back
Some states won't allow refugees
for fear of terrorist attacks
or in their words, "The U.S. not wanting Syrian refugees here
is not based not on fear,
it is based on wisdom and knowledge.
We should admit only proven Christians."
How do they prove they are Christians?
Maybe they could swear their devotion
to crucifixes mounted at checkpoints?

A presidential candidate
wants to I.D. Muslim citizens
and shut down mosques
The black president is called a
"sissy," "wuss" and "petulant child"
(translation: updated Jim Crow terms for "boy")
He is called the first female president
for urging restraint
even though the terrorism in Europe
was done by home grown terrorists
Someone said to me,
"They don't consider the Syrians people.
They consider them contraband."
Which immigrant families have caused more terror
Syrian families or the Bush family?

When attacks happened in Lebanon
Nigeria, Kenya, Mali, Indonesia
and Burkina Faso
there were no national anthems sung,

no buildings lit up in those countries' colors,
no comparisons to 9-11,
no moments of silence,
no 24-hour news cycle
on CNN or MSNBC,
just their "experts"
who spend their lives in green rooms
sampling free doughnuts and coffee
instead of interviews with civilians
presidents, prime ministers,
or experts from the countries involved

Why is a life in France
worth more grief and anger
than a life in Nigeria, Mali
Kenya, Lebanon,
Indonesia and Burkina Faso?
Where are the world's candles,
the vigils, the anthem-singing,
the hash tags, the letters,
the flowers for these victims?

# Winter Border Sweater Tights

I found the Hue winter border sweater tights at the new
Nordstrom Rack in Emeryville
in November 2015
They are black with tiny white snowflakes
from the waist to the ankle
and large snowflakes wrapped around the ankle
The feet are solid black
They are made out of cotton, polyester,
nylon and spandex

This is my third favorite pair
of Hue's sweater tights
after the first pair I bought in 2007
with their dull gray, pink, red and black
thick striped pattern
and the hot pink, bright orange, purple, and black
skinny striped patterned pair
that I bought in 2010
I wear this pair
with my gray Nike hooded sweatshirt dress
and my Nike sneakers
They feel like sweatpants to me
They don't itch
like opaque nylon tights do

They are great on cold, damp, breezy days
when sweatpants and jeans aren't warm enough

After many warm winters
The 2018-2019 was cold and rainy
with temperatures in the forties and fifties
Now it is late April of 2019
I have stored them for next year
I am hoping the 2019-2020 winter season
will be just as cold
so I can wear them a lot

## For Antonio Ramos

Every time I drive by
the mural you were painting
on 35th and West Streets in Oakland
under the 580 Interstate Overpass
I hold my breath
like I do right before
I get poked with a needle
I can't look at the mural
because it is still too painful
because this was where you were killed

In my dream on January 11, 2016
I was lighting a candle in front of the section
you were painting
The vigil and funeral were long gone
I was crying
A lady was looking at me, worried
We were the only two there
I thanked you for being my lighting designer
for my Berkeley City College
final project video shoot
on November 15, 2013
I told you I was angry at the ICE agent
who left his gun in plain view in his car
so the young man who shot you

was able to grab it when he broke into that agent's car
That's how he robbed you of your camera
at gun point
when all you had was a paintbrush

You would still be alive today
Your parents wouldn't have lost a son,
your sister wouldn't have lost a brother
and all of your friends
would still get to hang out with you
The middle school students would still be able
to work on the "Self as Super Hero" Mural Project with you

I remember your stories
of your trip to Puerto Rico
You told me if I go
to visit El Yunque National Forest
up in the mountains
and to bathe in the hot springs
I remember some of the jokes
that you made in class
When I entered the City College Studio
to take another video production class in 2016
I felt your presence

In 2017, I saw the memorial
flowers and candles are still freshly kept
and when I finally got the courage
to look at your last project up close
and saw the lavender house
you were painting when you died
I felt your spirit again

# GQ

"All he needs is a top hat
to be a top cat"

He looks like a gentleman
ready for an evening on the town
wearing a full dress coat and tail
with white gloves,
and a round face with a
curled, long mustache

"All he needs is a top hat
to be a top cat"

The first time I saw him
was on June 6, 2013
He entered through a hole
in the wooden board fence
on the northwest corner of the garden
seeking shade
underneath the apple tree

"All he needs is a top hat
to be a top cat"

His white chest is pure fluff
During the sunset
his black face has blue tints
and the hair on his legs and back
have dark red highlights
like he put henna in his fur
His white chin is pronounced
and he looks at me
as the pupils in his bright green eyes
become slits,
a sign that he is frightened

"All he needs is a top hat
to be a top cat"

During Halloween of 2015
as I waited for the trick-or-treaters
He was sitting on the front porch
watching them approach
He noticed me staring at him
through the window of the front door
He stood up and slowly headed in my direction,
paused in front of the door,
nodded his head up and down
He tried to smell me through the window
Then, as the porch lights came on,
he ran down the stairs
into the darkness,
his very furry tail a blur
waving to the rhythm of his run

Lately GQ has stopped showing up
There's no way to know why or for how long
because it happened once before
I don't even know if he belongs to somebody
I had a dream where he came back

He was cleaning himself next to
the garden chairs and table
His back right leg bent all the way back
I said to him, "Where have you been?"
He gave me his usual look
then he jumped on the porch
passing me to get inside of the house
I grabbed him
The dream ended
I miss old fluffy face
how he stares at me differently
according to where he finds me
He adds excitement to the garden
It has been ten and a half months now
I keep checking for him everyday

# Ode to Fruit Loops

Part One

I have observed the Black Crowned Night Heron
since June of 2008
He flies in to the Lake Merritt aviary
and lands on the metal fence
He only has his left leg
He loves to have his photo taken
and sometimes winks at me
with his red eye

His daytime mood is subdued,
eyes half closed
as he looks around the aviary
But when an obese man comes
with his elementary school aged children
to feed the birds Fruit Loops,
He stretches out his neck,
fluffs up his white chest
and flaps his blue wings
letting out a loud, "wok"
as he does during his nighttime hunts
then flies with the Canadian geese, pigeons,
seagulls, common egrets
and American pelicans
to grab some of the Fruit Loops

Part Two

Man has long created strategies
to obtain his version of Fruit Loops
Like the heron he fluffs his chest
with a large mansion in the hills,
a BMW exclusive coupé,
a stay at the Sandals Resort in Jamaica
where he can golf, be massaged
and have a Piña Colada served by the pool
or take a Viking River cruise along the Danube
to view Bavarian castles
from the balcony of his room
Man likes to polish himself till he shines

# Beyond Pluto

We come from Planet 9
the new Neptune sized planet
beyond Pluto
Humans have already
set up shop here
preparing for when climate change
gets to the point where Earth
becomes uninhabitable
They already brought us Walmart, McDonalds and Target

With our bodies made of scales,
our long tails and our wings
of butterfly ink we head towards Earth
to study humans
in their original habitat

We land in a fancy neighborhood
in the northeastern United States
There is a party going on
Snow covers the ground
The camellia bushes
have yet to flower
Through the window
we watch kids running
in holiday outfits

A dog is barking
and a cat is perched
on an upstairs window sill

Guests are sitting on chocolate leather couches
eating pigs in a blanket
or crackers and cheese
from Trader Joe's
Some of the women
are in the kitchen cooking
the holiday ham, macaroni and cheese,
green beans flavored with bacon
and some butterscotch brownies
Most of the men are watching football
The women are wearing
cocktail dresses and heels
The men are in suits and ties
There is a lot of conversing
while classical music plays on the hosts'
iPod stereo tower system in the living room
*"My parents and I went all over*
*Europe this past summer, before I entered*
*high school"* a ninth grade girl tells the adults
*"Whenever we are in Paris we go to the Champs-Elysées.*
*We like to go to Tiffany & Co. They are in the States of course,*
*but there is nothing like saying*
*'I bought this on the Champs-Elysées,'"* a lady says
*"You are in high school?"* the lady asks the girl
*"Yes,"* the teen replies
*"Have you thought about colleges?"*
*"No."*
*"Our second oldest granddaughter is in a private high school.*
*She gets all A's and studies a lot. She is on the swim team. We*
*are thinking she is Harvard- or Yale-bound."*
*"Really? My son is hopefully off to Oxford. He goes to Dartmouth.*
*We want him to be the next Rachel Maddow."*

"*My daughter is studying architecture. We want her to be the next Frank Lloyd Wright.*"

"*My grandson is a structural engineer. He designs codes for airplanes, MRI machines, etc. That's doing something.*"

"*My son is the CEO of Boeing. He will take us to Planet Nine when climate change gets to be so bad that we can't live on Earth anymore. They already have mega stores for the planet.*"

"*Well we have a vehicle that can travel faster than the speed of light,*" we say

Everyone turns and looks at us

The kids stop running and stare at us, mouths agape

The teenage girl takes a picture of us with her iPhone 6

An old lady faints

We have had the last word

# Plantain

She didn't really like me, the plantain
until her Haitian friend invited her over to dinner
where the menu was
Haitian crab, shrimp and okra gumbo
collard greens,
tilapia, brown rice and me,
one of her native foods,
which she fried in her black Cuisinart pan

The friends sat down in the living room
in front of folded out tables
near the altar with a photo
of the hostess's parents
when they were young adults
and a wooden statue
seated with legs crossed
on the fireplace
Her friend displayed paintings, hanging
throughout the apartment, made
by students from different colleges
and universities
throughout the Bay Area
in which she served as their live subject
Her favorite is the large nude
displayed on the wall in the eastern

part of the room
Her friend's Arawak features
are distinctive
She is lying on her left side
with her head supported by her hand
The painting reminds her
of Frieda Kahlo

Another painting,
much smaller,
is of her standing upright
It looks like a Picasso in his Cubist period

She began to cut me up in pieces
She was thinking that I was sweet
like my cousin, the banana,
which she has each morning with her oatmeal
She was surprised that I was bitter

# Mulhouse, France

She first heard of Mulhouse in 1992
when she flew into EuroAirport
Basel Mulhouse Freiburg
on a Swissair propeller plane
to start a tour of Germany

She didn't know that many years later,
in 2015, she would actually visit Mulhouse
for an international conference
at the Université de Haute-Alsace
in the hills east of the town center

No cars are allowed in the town center
At twilight she walks cobblestoned streets
from the Hotel Kyriad Mulhouse Centre
past the towering steeple on Saint Stephen's Protestant Church,
a gray stone Gothic Revival renovation from the 19th century,
contrasting with a 19th-century carousel's brightly painted horses, lions
and garlanded benches waiting for riders to appear
surrounded by orange, yellow, pink and turquoise
apartment buildings whose street level shop windows
sport mannequins modeling spring wear:
floral blouses, white sports jackets and blue jeans
even though it is only forty degrees outside
and spring is not yet a week old

She arrives at the pink and red 1553 Old Town Hall
with the flag of France hanging in front
Inside, terra cotta columns support
the chevron patterned wood ceiling
Its knots remind her of homes in Santa Fe

Upstairs in the corridor the windows
with their diamond shaped panes
made of glass and lead
allow her a clear view of the town center
The trompe l'oeil painted ceilings
remind her of Julia Morgan's detailing
at the Berkeley City Club
and the Wells Fargo Bank on College and Ashby

In the late evening
the sky looks a charcoal gray
instead of midnight black
as she heads back to the hotel
The lamps attached to upper floors of apartment buildings
cast everything in bright yellow, gold and caramel
except the steeples of Saint Stephen's
shadowed in the background
and a special street lamp, which captures
the arched, stained glass windows of the church

The shops are closed
yet their lights remain on
turning the cobblestones bright white
Few people walk down the narrow street
The completeness of this scene is something
she could not find in the States

# The Dream

She was four or five
and at the home of her
after school care taker
She was sitting at the
kitchen table
waiting for her snack

The plastic tablecloth
was teal green
with printed lemons
The walls were shamrock green
and aureolin
"Maple Leaf Rag" by Scott Joplin
was playing on the radio

She was playing with her Barbie
The Barbie had hip length hair, stud earrings,
a long one-shoulder dress
and plastic high heels
The little girl wanted really long hair
and pierced ears for herself
She thought girls didn't look good with short hair
and ears that weren't pierced

As she was served tea
the little girl noticed the bright walls
They gave her a headache
She started crying
"What's wrong?" the caretaker asked
The dream ends

# "Post-Racism"

"Post-Racism,"
People say,
"We have a Black president.
Racism is over."

"Post-Racism"
Someone at a daycare center says,
"Discrimination towards Black people
is based on class, not on race."

"Post-Racism"
A student in a sound design class
makes a video with Robert Kennedy's eulogy
for Martin Luther King
 as voiceover for the ape scene in
"2001 Space Odyssey"
Another student does a storyboard
involving African men being drunk and abusive
Someone in the same class names their villain "Mohammed"
For this character they use an image of the guy
who shot 36 people in San Bernardino

"Post-Racism"
People on Facebook and media panelists believe
"Support of Trump has nothing to do
with Obama being Black or a Harvard graduate
It has to do with them thinking
the country is headed in the wrong direction."

This is how we got Trumped

## Alton Sterling and Philando Castile

Alton Sterling and Philando Castile
killed in front of their children

Alton Sterling and Philando Castile
shot for selling CDs and a broken taillight while Black

Alton Sterling and Philando Castile
both had concealed weapons permits
Why is the NRA remaining silent?
Because those laws only protect White people
who want to shop at Walmart,
get coffee at Starbucks
and attend the Republican National Convention
Even the Louisiana and Minnesota governors
say that if Sterling and Castile were White
they wouldn't have been shot

Alton Sterling and Philando Castile
Their children have to grow up without a father

Alton Sterling and Philando Castile
Thank God for YouTube,
Facebook Live, Twitter, Instagram,
Snapchat and Pinterest

Alton Sterling and Philando Castile
The White liberal go-to lines
showing up on Facebook and other social media sites
object that we are "playing the race card,"
and we have "reverse racism towards the cops,"
or "not everything is about race,"
and "Black on Black crime
is a higher statistic than
White cops killing Black people.
Why don't you talk about that?"
and anyway, "All Lives Matter."

Alton Sterling and Philando Castile
Someone I know observed,
"The police are asking for warfare in this country.
Black people aren't going to take this much longer."
On July 7, 2016, people protest in Oakland, California;
New York City; Washington, D.C.; Chicago;
Saint Paul, Minnesota; Baton Rouge, Louisiana;
and Dallas, Texas
Protestors vandalize a police station
and block the I-880 freeway in Oakland for hours
In Washington, D.C. they shout over
Congressmen John Lewis
On CNN the protestors are told to remain peaceful
Why don't they say that to the police?
During the next week
five police officers are killed
and seven are injured by a sniper
near El Centro College in Dallas
In Baton Rouge three cops are killed

Guns don't kill, people do?

# Wednesday, November 9, 2016

*"Never underestimate the stupidity of the American voter."*

Ishmael Reed.

Was I dreaming?

Circles under my eyes
and two more silver hairs

The Tea Party,
the Green Party,
and the Green Tea Party
Those who didn't vote
Those who didn't care

Inner racism, inner misogyny,
inner xenophobia, inner Islamophobia,
inner anti-Semitism, inner homophobia
inner classism

Slavery, internment camps,
exclusion acts, stolen lands, deportation,
"locker room talk"
Disinformation, FBI probes, WikiLeaks,
Putin's fake news troll farms, birthers, gerrymandering

A throwback cracker for attorney general
who wants to get rid of Affirmative Action
an education secretary
who wants to get rid of Special-Ed,
a Supreme Court judge who supports
excessive force from police,
an EPA director who denies climate change
an energy secretary who did not know
he would be in charge of supervising all things nuclear
Homeland Security even stops Syrian immigrants with visas
when they arrive seeking asylum from the war
but instead find themselves detained or deported
even though the Secretary of Homeland Security wouldn't be here
without immigration
Young Mexican and Central American children
are handcuffed at border crossings
stranded under detention in a strange country
without their parents to comfort them

Latino students are taunted by their classmates,
"I guess you have to move."
An email from my college advises students
with student visas and Green Cards
not to leave the United States
An email from another college instructs teachers
on how not to offend pro-Trump students

My friends not believing
that forty-four percent of college educated White women
voted for Trump
I respond, "That's their White privilege and elitism."

The White left is as racist
as the White right
but instead of being on the red end of the rainbow
they're on the violet end of the rainbow

What a way to end my thirties
and begin my forties
As a woman in her sixties apologized to me,
"My generation messed things up
for your generation"
Let's hope that the Democrats
controlling the House
will weaken the Trump presidency
from a hurricane to a low pressure system
and will eventually go out to sea in 2020

# I Have Worn It For Over Thirty Years

Guess, that is
I was nine, almost ten,
early February of 1987
We had just arrived in Massachusetts
We were going to live on the edge
of Cambridge, in Somerville
for three and a half months
While my parents started their work at Harvard,
and searched for an elementary school for me,
a late family friend took me
to Filene's Department Store in Wellesley
We found a sky blue short-sleeved Guess logo tee shirt
that said "GUESS PARIS" in black
and had a large, yellow question mark
surrounded by three yellow polka dots
placed inside a black upside down equilateral triangle
The tee shirt came with two cotton, ribbed turtlenecks
One white, one yellow
I took the tee shirt with me to Martinique
at the end of 1987,
the turtlenecks to London in 1989
The turtlenecks lasted until I was thirteen,
the tee shirt until I was fifteen
I haven't had a Guess turtleneck since then
but I have tons of Guess logo tees

In the summer of 1987
a teenage family friend in Berkeley handed down to me
her standard 1981 high rise skinny jeans in stone wash
They had a button fly and a large,
white upside down equilateral triangle applique
on the back, right pocket
that said "GUESS USA WASHED JEANS 1201 1203"
a classic jean that I saw actors/actresses wear
on eighties and nineties sitcoms like "Full House,"
"Roseanne" and "A Different World"
I wore that hand-me-down 1981 pair
on my middle school trip to Arizona
at summer camp and to school
all the way through tenth grade
Now, thirty years later,
I still look for the equilateral triangle
and I still wear their iconic
1981 high-rise skinny jeans
Jennifer Lopez sported them
in the Spring 2018 edition
of "Guess" Magazine
She is almost ten years older than me
so they are targeting
women my age

I have worn it for over thirty years,
Guess that is,
Ages 9-42
1987-2019
My current most dressy favorites are
a black silk blouse and black pencil skirt
They come from Marciano, the Guess top line
I call them my "business suit"

I recently found out the founders of Guess are Moroccan-born Jews
who immigrated to Los Angeles the year I was born
I always wondered why they named their brand GUESS
The story goes they got the idea from a McDonald's billboard
asking drivers to guess
which eatery offered the biggest cheeseburger

# Ode to the Vegan

Vegangelizing,
that's how I describe vegans
who shove their cause into meat eaters' faces
the way they accuse meat eaters
of shoving our cause into their faces

They want conferences
and hospital cafeterias
to offer only one hundred percent vegan fare
or in their words,
"Everyone can eat vegan food;
not everyone can or wants to eat meat."
Have they never considered the possibility that
not everybody wants to or can be vegan?
What about all the junk food consumed righteously
because it can be called vegan?
What about diabetics or pre-diabetics
who can't have a carbohydrate overload?
What about poor people or homeless people
who can't pick and choose what they eat?
To those of us not part of the vegan cult,
veganism is a privilege and a fashion
not based on health and ethics

Poets and lecturers compare practices of meat eaters
to slavery and the Holocaust
even though these animals are a different "animal"
than victims of slavery and the Holocaust
If we don't think their way we are called "speciesists"
Slaves and Holocaust victims were killed because of their identity
Animals are killed because their meat tastes good
and are a primary source of protein
and the means for many to survive
Animals eat other animals
Are they like Nazis and slave owners, too?

Do vegans not realize that plants feel pain?
Is it because plants don't have ears
even though they can hear themselves being eaten?
Is it because they don't look you in the eye
when you dry them off from the rain
or wag their tail when they see you?
Is it because they don't sit in your lap and purr
or respond when you talk to them?

I wonder what the people
in the Somalian famine think of this?
#firstworldproblems

# Viaggio Italiano

*(Italian Travel)*
*(Sequel to Nihon No Ryokō)*

You can't always take the combo
American Airlines/British Airways flights to Rome
Sometimes you find a better airline
at a cheaper price
like Turkish Airlines
with courteous flight attendants,
their standard amenity kit
with socks, slippers, ear buds,
toothpaste, an eye mask
and a personal chef who offers you
salmon and omelet dishes

Once you've landed you can't always find American food
but you learn the pizza and tiramisu
in Treviso is better than those served in the States
and the calamari fresh from the lagoon in Venice
is much better than the fried calamari
at the Westfield Mall in San Francisco

You won't always stay in one place
all the time
Sometimes you take the .italo train

round trip from Rome to Florence in one day
and then from Rome to Venice one way the next
plus the regional train to Treviso
and a cab to Vicenza

You might not locate the leather wallets
you were told could once be found
outside the Uffizi Gallery in Florence
Now you can find them
at a hole-in-the-wall shop in Venice

Sometimes you run into glitches
like a track problem on the .italo train
that delays you for an hour
or you get off at Venice/Maestra
one stop before the end of the line at Venice/Santa Lucia

You can't always stay in a hotel room
like those in the fourteenth century palace
Hotel Foresteria Levi
facing the Grand Canal
with an interior courtyard
and a room lit by a glass chandelier made in Murano
hanging from a wood beamed ceiling
Sometimes you have to stay at the Best Western in Rome
because the price was right
whose rude concierge
calls you a cab that takes you to the Coliseum
in thirty-five minutes instead of fifteen minutes
and who throws out your laundry

Luckily you won't find the U.S. everywhere
but you can find ancient ruins
that were once government buildings in Rome,
a Bernini fountain centerpiece for a neighborhood's roundabout,
the oldest Jewish Ghetto in Europe still active late at night,

the pope speaking to a packed crowd on Sunday in Saint Peter's Square,
the Vatican Museum's painted fresco ceilings,
the crowds studying the ceiling at the Sistine Chapel,
where Michelangelo's "The Creation of Adam" is the star,
the tallest dome in the world
also designed by Michelangelo capping Saint Peter's Basilica,
a luminescent "The Birth of Venus"
with her long, red hair afloat at the Uffizi in Florence,
where the Cathedral of Santa Maria de Fiore
took two centuries to complete,
a marble David with his cracking ankle stars at the Academia Gallery,
Dante's thirteenth century home, now a museum for his life mask, costumes
and spare writing loft beneath wood beamed eaves,
motorboat rides along Venice's Grand Canal,
walks along narrow cobblestone calli,
Peggy Guggenheim's eighteenth century villa
where she lies, her fourteen dogs, aka her "beloved babies,"
buried alongside her in the back palazzo's garden
and her dining room's polished dark wood furniture still intact,
its walls hung with Picasso's "The Poet"
and Duchamp's "Sad Young Man on a Train,"
San Marco Square with its Middle Eastern looking basilica
and campanile that reveals where U.C. Berkeley got its inspiration,
a Saturday morning farmer's market
with fresh fish, cheese, gigantic vegetables and chocolates in Treviso
and the Rococo Palazzo Leoni Montanari in Vicenza
with the largest Russian religious art collection outside of Russia
before getting up at 4:00 a.m.
to catch your Turkish Airlines flight
out of Venice/Marco Polo Airport

# You Can't Only Call Them White Nationalists

They don't care
about twenty six year old schoolchildren killed in Sandy Hook
the five hundred forty-seven victims of mass shooting in Las Vegas
or the seventeen students, teachers and staff killed in Parkland,
Florida
because the NRA controls them
Like atomic bomb drills
for their grandparents' generation,
lock down drills are these children's new norm

They don't care
about the millions of Americans who won't have health insurance
or who won't receive food stamps,
the millions of senior citizens
who will lose Medicare, Medicaid
and Social Security
and who will potentially be kicked out of nursing homes
for lack of funds
or about women who won't be able to afford
prenatal care, screenings for cancer,
or testing for AIDS
because they cut funding to Planned Parenthood
They say they are pro-life
but once the child is out of the womb
they stay hands off
Everyone's on their own

They don't care
that poor people will have to pay proportionately more
in taxes than rich people
and young people who can't afford to go to college
or take on major debt because of college
may not find appropriate jobs after college

They don't care
about those who lost everything in Harvey, Irma, Maria
and the California wildfires, floods and mudslides
or about future generations
who will live with the consequences
of denying climate change
They say they want to keep the focus
on "Pittsburgh not Paris"
but neither Pittsburgh nor Paris
would be exempt from climate change

They don't care
if there will be serious international consequences
when they call other countries s***holes
They choose to remain silent
even when there's a threat of nuclear extinction

They care
about their donors, the one-percent,
who paid billions
of tax deductible campaign dollars
to ensure they can keep their lifestyles up
and now we indulge a First Family
who travel on separate planes
and in separate motorcades
at we, the taxpayers, expense
because they can't stand to be around each other

# NOLA

Part One: September 2016

While horse drawn carriages await them
tourists meander down Decatur Street
in the September heat
and step inside Café du Monde
to cool down and enjoy
coffee laced with chicory
accompanied by beignet mix

Barges slide along the Mississippi River
towards the Crescent City bridge
Fans arrive from all over the country
to watch the Raiders and Saints football game
at the Mercedes-Benz Superdome
where nothing indicates
9,000 Katrina evacuees were housed there
as a "shelter of the last resort"

Along with local musicians playing
tuba, trumpet and trombone in Jackson Square
in front of Saint Louis Cathedral
you can sing,
"No one here can love or understand me
Oh, what hard luck stories they all hand me

Pack up all my cares and woe, here I go, winging low
Bye, bye, blackbird"


Part Two: January 2018


Weather alerts predict an ice storm will arrive in the evening
causing a hard freeze
That doesn't stop us from finding Congo Square
now called Louis Armstrong Park
north of the French Quarter,
where eighteenth and nineteenth century Black people,
both free and enslaved operated open markets,
held meetings, and African dance
and drumming celebrations
and where cultural and musical events carry on those traditions
today
Crows caw from the massive live oak tree
Otherwise the space is completely empty
We see no mention on site that this is where
Africans were routinely bought and sold
During the mini ice storm,
followed by a hard freeze,
the whole city shuts down
unused to these conditions
No restaurants are open
schools are closed,
people are told to stay off roads,
no one is even walking around,
outdoor music events are postponed,
all flights are cancelled
A boiling water alert is issued
after pipes become frozen and burst
People are warned not to drink tap water,
not to bathe in hotel tubs, especially infants and children,
not to brush their teeth in the sinks

and to sanitize hands
after washing them

When things slowly return to normal
the French Quarter still barely has foot traffic
People stay warm
at the Astor Crowne Plaza Hotel's
Dickie Brennan's Bourbon House & Seafood Bar
where they order Old Fashioned Oatmeal
with brown sugar and seasonal fruit
and Greek Yogurt Parfait
with house made granola
The Pontchartrain Expressway to Louis Armstrong Airport
finally reopens,
but TSA agents announce the restrooms aren't operating past
security
Frustrated passengers board
Virgin America Flight No. 1391 bound for SFO
who were supposed to depart the day before
They stand in the back of the plane waiting to use the bathrooms
and then find their seats
happy to finally head home

# My Last Poem About Plastic Shoes

I have published poems
about the plastic shoes known as jellies
in almost all of my previous poetry collections
This will be my last poem about jellies
and my obsession of
the replacing of replacements of replacements
since I was three years old

I have owned about fifty pairs of jellies
within the last thirty-nine years
in a variety of styles:
t-strap sandals, fisherman sandals, gladiator sandals,
ballet flats, latticed flats, huarache flats,
wedge heels, clunky heels, platforms,
flip-flops, slides, sneakers, rain boots and Mary Janes
I used to cry when my jellies would crack and break
and I would tape them up with duct tape
trying to hang on to them as long as I could
but they have become sturdier and more expensive
as the years go by so they last longer
Now I own four pairs
My latest and greatest
are sparkly gold ballet flats,
fisherman sandals,
sneakers

and rain booties
all by the Brazilian brand Melissa
I have wanted Melissa jellies for years

I swear this is my final ode to jellies

# My First Poem about Nike Sneakers

Long revealing my obsession with plastic shoes,
since my first book of poetry,
this is my first poem about Nike sneakers

As I write this poem
I have a flashback
to almost thirty-four years ago
I got my first pair of Nike sneakers
when I was entering third grade,
the 1985-86 year at LeConte Elementary School in Berkeley
They were a pair of lavender Velcro sneakers
with a white swoosh
I wore them almost every day to school
They went with everything

From 2014 through 2018 my favorite style
was the Nike Air Max Tailwind sneaker
I had owned four pairs
in a variety of colors
They were great for my back
I wore them almost every day
like I did with my third grade pair
I hung onto my last Tailwind pair as long as I could
They bit the dust in April of 2019
Now my new favorite is

the Vapormax sneaker
as the Tailwind sneaker is discontinued,
an idea I got from a Berkeley High School student
walking down Center Street with her friends
I have seen them all over New York City as well
They are very comfortable
and have a jelly sole,
which is what attracted me to them
I wear them with everything, but I love to wear them
with my Nike apparel: sweatpants, hoodies, pullovers,
tee shirts and dresses

I am relieved to say Nike has responded to campaigns
exposing their sweatshop scandal of 1997/1998
Since I can't make such shoes myself
and because I believe all global brands
are equally as guilty of child labor and
factories run with near slavery like conditions
sometimes I feel political correctness demands go too far

# A Haiku to the Super Blue Blood Moon

Super blue blood moon
I had to wake up at four
Lots of Facebook likes

# Barcelona Haiku

Narrow gothic streets
Gaudi ventilation shafts
Crowds on La Rambla

# Spring 2018

It means the earth is beginning to tilt
causing each hemisphere to warm
and plants to grow
It means March through June in the Northern Hemisphere
and September to December in the Southern Hemisphere

It was warmer in February
than in May
so I went back to wearing
turtlenecks, sweatsuits, jeans,
parkas, hats and scarves

Gray, gloomy days and still rain
Frequent flight delays at SFO
Everyone complained to the KPIX 5 meteorologist
who said Spring would come by Memorial Day,
the unofficial start to Summer
People picnicked at Lake Temescal, Lake Merritt
and the Emeryville Marina
Our neighbors had barbeques
in their backyards
and the air carried
the sounds of many conversations and music
There were tanks, shorts and sandals,
wide brim hats and sunglasses

Only for it to get cool again
two days later

Springtime means unpredictable weather:
In New York City and Paris
it means transitioning from snowstorms to thunderstorms
in Barcelona it means warm, sunny days
turning to cool, rainy nights
In Buffalo it means sixty-four degrees one day
and snow the next
In Venice and Rome it means
rain one day and sun the next
In Alabama and Tennessee
it means going from forty-degrees and snow one week
to eighty-degrees the next
It means the beginning of wildfires in the West
and the beginning of hurricane season in the Atlantic and Gulf
Coast
The cherry blossoms begin to bloom
at U.C. Berkeley and La Loma Park
There are the cherry blossom festivals
in San Francisco, Washington, D.C. and Japan

People begin to travel by car, rail and air
for Spring Vacation, Passover, Easter and Memorial Day
The security lines at airports get longer and slower
and the planes are packed full of families

It means the N.B.A. playoffs, semi-finals and finals
and the beginning of baseball season
Sometimes the Warriors and A's play at the same time
at the Oracle Arena and the O.co Coliseum

Springtime means graduations
from pre-school, elementary, middle and high school,
college, masters and doctoral programs
It means college acceptance letters

Spring turns into Summer
officially with the longest day of the year

# Cancer

It takes too many lives

I have lost friends/colleagues/classmates to cancer:
lung, ovarian, bile duct, abdominal and brain
Three schoolmates have battled cancer
All of these people are/were in
their early forties through their seventies
The ones who died left behind
young children and adult children, grandchildren,
spouses, parents, brothers and sisters,
uncles and aunts, grandparents,
pets, friends and colleagues
Some didn't know they had it until too late
because they waited too long to get a check-up
and some because initially there had been a misdiagnosis

Two family members had prostate cancer,
one had testicular cancer,
two others basal cell
and one non-Hodgkin Lymphoma twice
I had Melanoma
We were all lucky to survive,
but still suffer the consequences
We have to have check-ups,
be careful of exposure to germs,

deal with neuropathy,
wear hats and sunblock,
all the while worrying if it will happen again

Because cancer has been with us
for as far back as we know
In 2016 a relative of modern humans who died 1.6-1.8 million
years ago
was found in the South African Swartkrans Cave
with osteosarcoma in a toe bone,
one of the most aggressive types of cancer
And an Egyptian papyri from 1600 BCE documents that
during the 2700th century BCE
the great Imhotep, the pharaoh's physician and architect
of Saqqara's step pyramid
who later was deified as a god
treated eight cases of tumors of the breast
So looks like this is just part of the deal, folks

# Life Lessons from the Peanut Gallery

Starting when I was a child
I have been told to be assertive
when people pushed me around
and also counseled that I needed to be more self-aware,
since if everyone was the same
the world would be a boring place,
and "Not everyone is going to like you,"
lessons I didn't start understanding
until my mid-thirties

In my teens I was confronted with the ugly charges
"diarrhea of the mouth," and "chatterbox"
yet I could argue the same for people
who would ask me in my twenties
"Do you have a boyfriend?" or
"What are you?"
or pronounce, "If you marry a Black man,
a Jewish man, a White man,
or an Indian man,
your child will be more Black, Jewish,
White or Indian than anything else"
or "If you marry a man who doesn't
have learning disabilities, one child will have
learning disabilities and the other won't"
I was informed that when people asked these questions

or made these comments
they were usually talking to themselves
as ninety percent of people's behaviors
had nothing to do with me
Or were they offering lessons on probability theory?
These kinds of questions stopped
once I reached my late twenties

Instead throughout my thirties, people would ask me,
"Who do you think is a better writer, you or your dad?"
My stock answer: "We write differently"
That question stopped in my late thirties

Now I am in my early forties
and the question about having kids
has come up again
as I begin the transition into menopause
When I tell them I don't think I will be having kids
people say, "Well my friend had kids in their forties"
and, "There are all sorts of tests to lessen the risks"
When I complain
about grocery store clerks at Berkeley Bowl and Safeway
who tell me, when I ask for assistance,
that I look "young and strong enough"
to lift my own bags from the counter to the cart
even though I have had low back pain
for twelve years now
I am advised, "Why worry about these people?
They don't have the power to do anything to you."
or, "You will hardly cross paths ever again,"
or "If you expect less from people you'll be a happier person,"
or "In order to have extraordinary you have to have ordinary"
Some tell me, "I stopped caring what others thought of me when
I turned fifty."
Hopefully I will internalize that lesson before reaching fifty
comforted by one person's observation

that humans have only been on two legs
for fifty thousand years
or accepting of the consequences
that humans may prove to be an evolutionary error
I don't suffer fools gladly

# Thoughts In My Forties

An early fortieth birthday present
the day after Trump was elected
was a diagnosis of pre-diabetes

Unlike a woman in the Kaiser Permanente
pre-diabetes class
who brags that she doesn't have to lose weight
but admits she doesn't want to give up
Starbucks Grande Caffé Mocha,
I have to watch my blood sugar
Now I set limits on my chocolate cravings
or eat fruit or sugar free desserts
(which have come to taste better to me)
Whole grain chips and crackers are my snacks
Instead of Sprite at restaurants
ginger mint tea or water are my beverages

Eleven months later,
thanks to my discipline
of cutting way back on sugar and processed foods,
drinking a lot of water,
keeping steady with exercising
and losing the excess weight,
I got out of the pre-diabetes range
I think the diagnosis was a blessing
It inspired me to change my habits

On my fortieth birthday,
February 28, 2017,
someone told me that I look eighteen
When people think
you look like a teenager
they are often condescending
Although at least one friend commiserated
about this "unsolicited advice"
when I explained how it bothers me
most people continue to advise
"It's a compliment,"
or "you'll like hearing this when you're older"

But I'm sure I don't want to revisit raging hormones,
persistent acne,
senior year of high school,
high school general education courses,
figuring out what college to go to,
freshman year of college,
and repeating those same required courses in college,
peer pressure, meanness from my classmates,
and enduring run of the mill teenage junk: the stupidity, silliness,
poor choices, hot headedness,
and trying to figure out who I want to be
Fortunately, now that I am forty-one,
I haven't heard that comment much lately

I have done a lot for a person that reached their forties
I've earned my ten silver hairs
and now fight gravity
Eighteen was twenty-four years ago
Keep it that way

# California Burning
## 2017-2018


I am thinking back to October 9, 2017
around 4:30AM in North Oakland
My window was open
What smelled like someone barbecuing
or burning wood
was the Tubbs Fire igniting
Santa Rosa, Napa and Lake counties
Caused by Eucalyptus trees,
an Australian import,
when one fell into a PG&E power line
it fulfilled their firebombing menace
Friends of mine had to evacuate
with their fourteen-month-old
and a second on the way
Another only had time to grab her dog
and put him in the back of her pick-up truck

Smoke followed me to my classroom
at Berkeley City College
At Kaiser Permanente
patients visiting internal medicine wore masks
They did so in the lab as well
At the end of the day
I walked with my neighbor

and her Border Collie/Australian Shepherd mix dog
in the landmark Mountain View Cemetery
In spite of the sun's brilliant red
San Francisco was barely visible in the distance from the haze
She is a restaurateur whose employer planned to send her
to replenish Sonoma winery stock
She was not sure the trip would happen
Later on she reported that some of her co-workers
lost everything in the Tubbs Fire
I think about how that hot, dry October of 2017
was not like October of 2016
when early rains kept fires away

As each fire area was discovered it was named
to aid the firefighters' planning logistics
The Lions, Hot Creek, County,
Owens and Donnell fires
were among the fifty-eight fires
named in 2018
breaking records for burning the most acreage
in California history

Two combined into one
named the River and Ranch Fires
became the state's largest ever recorded
It burned for fifty-four days
forcing tens of thousands
to leave their homes
The fire acquired consciousness when
"It created its own wind"

Much of Yosemite National Park was closed
due to the Ferguson fire
sending vacationers to Mammoth Lake,
Sequoia and King's Canyon National Parks instead
We lost some of the thousand year old "wonders,"

the giant sequoias at Mariposa Grove
that I walked amongst in 2012
Fire warnings even reached the Lake Tahoe area

The Carr fire in Shasta County,
caused by a car failure,
was the second deadliest fire of 2018
My middle school teacher, Gloria,
who lives in Redding, reported on Facebook
that she was okay
although smoke surrounded her
The news report said it was 113 degrees
and there was no humidity

People's eyes burned from the haze,
their noses bled and they coughed
Asthma conditions worsened
Even cats were not immune
Cars were dusted in ash
When smoky air reached the East Bay
people chose daily walks around bay trails
because air quality seemed better
than in the hills
Governor Jerry Brown called this the "new normal"

Trump tweeted that water that could be used
to fight the fires is
"foolishly being diverted into the Pacific Ocean"
Was he suggesting that waters run from the ocean to the
mountains?
The Camp fire of November 2018
destroyed Paradise,
the town Trump called "Pleasure"

In Butte County alone,
eighty-six people have been recorded as dead

and three are still unaccounted for
A Norovirus outbreak hit shelters
sickening 145 people
and people slept in their cars out in the cold
The air quality was so bad in the Bay Area
that we were told to stay indoors,
schools were closed,
cable cars were shut down
and people scrambled to find masks
at local drug and hardware stores
We had the worst air pollution ranking on Earth
surpassing Delhi, Beijing, Istanbul, Moscow,
Buenos Aires, Paris and Los Angeles
This went on for almost two weeks
We finally got relief from the rain

Will smoke days become the West's new snow days?
When an early morning dagger of red light
cuts through my curtains
I think of what I want to save
in case I have to evacuate

# Look Before You Leap

"These works always propose a picture plane that
directs the viewer towards a deeper interior. Maybe
the quintessential work in this series is 'Descent Into
Limbo,' which is a hole in the ground. It reads not like
a hole in the ground, but like a black carpet sitting on
the floor. It is not an empty dark space, but a space
full of darkness."

Anish Kapoor.


I first heard of this story via Facebook
on August 20, 2018

Monday, August 13, 2018
A sixty something year old man from Italy
visits Anish Kapoor's *Descent Into Limbo*
an outdoor installation of an oval shaped hole
inside the form of a freestanding concrete and stucco cube
about twenty square feet
at the Fundação de Serralves
Museum of Contemporary Art in Porto, Portugal
Before entering the cube
everyone is asked to sign a disclaimer
alerting them to the risk involved
Signs warn people not to come too close
to the jet black oval shaped hole in the center of the room

that is so opaque it appears to have no depth
One visitor describes looking inside the circle
as a "dizzying experience"
Guards surround the site watching for visitors
who might wish to test if it is no more
than a trick of the eye

The mystery is achieved through
Vantablack, a material, not a paint
described as "the blackest black on the planet"
because it absorbs light and radiation
Warfare ignites on social media about who can use the tool
as Kapoor has secured an exclusive license
from Surrey NanoSystems
a British aerospace, engineering and optics research facility
who says, "It is often described as the closest thing
to a black hole we'll ever see"

Kapoor's followers on Instagram write,
"My first encounter, stays in my memory forever"
"Don't get yourself sucked,"
"Spooky,"
"Looney Tunes,"
"Amazing,"
while the warring party maintains "#sharetheblack"

The sixty-year-old man
is evidently so compelled to stare into the abyss
to discover if the pit has a bottom
he falls eight feet down
ripping the sides off of the installation
Making a hole within a hole
he definitively destroys the illusion of infinity
for everyone
The man injures his back, requiring a hospital stay
Luckily, he didn't die

The exhibit is temporarily closed for repairs
The work becomes an international art world cause celeb
digitally crossing into fame through popular culture and print
media
which is when I found out about it

# Llamas are the New Unicorns

They moved out of my dreams and into my living room
where there's a gold llama lamp base from Cost Plus
with a gold fern shade on top,
a hand-made llama mug and dish from West Elm,
a llama throw blanket found on Amazon
and don't forget the miniature carved wooden llama
that my late grandmother brought back from South America,
housed on a shelf of my tall, white bookcase
with its donkey friend
and my miniature llama made out of llama wool,
an end of school year gift from my fifth grade teacher
My books on animals are behind them
Then there's the Ecuadorian wall hanging
with a shepherd, llama and four ducks
woven with llama wool
hanging on my closet door
that I found in a Cambridge, Massachusetts street fair
when I was ten
 As a kid I loved Sesame Street's song,
"Me and My Llama," sung by a seven-year-old girl
as she took her llama along to the dentist
That's how long I have loved them
I've even ridden a llama in New Hampshire,
fed them at a Marin County farm
and Marine World in Vallejo

and had recurring dreams
of two of them at an imaginary farm in Tilden Park,
one a light cream color and the other a walnut brown
standing by a wooden lattice shaped fence
watching me as we drove by
with two sets of large, dark brown eyes
on each side of a wide, straight nose

Now I am not alone
At Marshalls you could pick-up
"Save the Drama for Your Llama" pillows
and black llama print Christmas themed leggings
Macy's sells llama hats for infants,
Nordstrom's Rack has llama socks (I have two pairs),
and Target has llama sheets for kids
Online you could buy llama shower curtains, doormats and
dusters,
"Fa La La La Llama" and "Happy Llamakah" sweaters
and llama cakes, cookies and wine glasses
My neighbor gave me a llama water bottle for Christmas
and a llama toiletries bag she brought back from Chile
I succumbed to red flannel llama pajama pants online from the Gap
After those pajamas no more llamas

Cal imports therapy llamas for Llamapalooza
to help students de-stress during "dead week"
Llamas pop up all over U.C. Berkeley's Instagram page
where students smile as they pet them, feed them carrots
and take selfies
But sometimes the llamas' ears are down,
a sign that they're not happy
The students can't resist those banana shaped ears,
the long eyelashes and their "smile"
I personally love the necks
I hope to see them at Memorial Glade one day

# Holiday Specials

The holiday season is here
On the Monday before Thanksgiving
the parking lot is full
as people stand online
to buy honey baked ham
Most have mobility issues
An obese woman waddles to her car
carrying two bags full of dextrose, brown sugar,
sodium phosphates, sodium nitrate,
sodium diacetate and corn syrup
An observer says, "If they're so big
that they can hardly walk up two stairs
maybe they shouldn't be buying
honey baked ham."
His friend replies,
"I'm not saying nothin'.
I'm not saying a goddamn thing."

Then there is the Chocolate Wonderfall
at Golden Corral
a.k.a. "Listeria on a Stick"
a.k.a. a spinning waterfall of Diabetes
One kid sticks his hands in
and another sticks her doll's head into
this lava of germs and dust

where people dip their marshmallows,
cookies and berries

A lesson about holiday cheer
to last throughout the new year

# 2018 Contemplation

## (*Parody of James Tate's Last Poem*)

I sat at my desk and contemplated all that I had accomplished in 2018. I was accepted to the Rockefeller Foundation's Bellagio Center residency for my poetry. No, I wasn't. I was just kidding. My manuscript was accepted by Harper Collins. False. I got business class on my trip to New York. In my dreams. I got to meet actress Amy Adams. Wow! I got to see a bear. Yummie! I got to go to Prague. Can you believe it? I reinjured my low back. Ouch! I slowly began to rehabilitate myself. It was tiring. I went home and slept for two hours. Awake! I set a record for swimming from one end of the Hearst Pool to the other. Blurb. I discovered an autobiography written by my late cat who died in 1996. Great! I slept all the way from San Francisco to London. Whew! I ate a Kit Kat bar every day for a year. I never want to do that again. A dog bit me at Golden Bear track. I couldn't catch her. I visited the city where my grandmother used to live and didn't recognize it. That's how long it's been. A policeman pulled me over to scan my disabled placard. He had his hand on his holster. He apologized. He noticed it was legit. What are the chances?

# Flight Attendant

*(Parody of Clarence Major's "Supply and Demand")*


As a flight attendant
for a major U.S. carrier
I lasted thirty years.
The life of a flight attendant
is not what you see on TV shows like "Pan Am."
The starting pay was lousy.
I had to move far from home after training.
I had to stay in a crash pad with twenty other girls
where I had no privacy
and had to share a kitchen and bathroom
because it was the most affordable.
I often missed holidays with family
because I had to work.
I couldn't schedule visits with friends
because I didn't have a consistent work schedule.
But I could walk through the terminal in high heels,
keep a smile on my face for a long time,
and keep up with food and drink orders.
I had to work four flights in one day
and only got paid when the doors were closed.
When I got to my final destination
I often forgot where I was.
My sleeping, eating and work out patterns

were always messed up.
As I got older, my body protested even more.
Sometimes I got airsick
when I sat in my jump seat
in a cramped galley during turbulence.
The airlines went bankrupt after 9-11
and we had to fight to keep our pensions.
We won that fight.
There was a hiring freeze.
Even though I made lifelong friendships
with some of my crew,
I was lucky enough
where if I didn't get along with them,
there was often a slim to none possibility
of me working with them again.
Then I was assigned a new position: "janitor."
One less person to pay $15 per hour, right?
Sometimes I had a melt down at the airport
in front of my child when I had to travel non-rev
because all of the direct flights were booked
and I had to travel all over the country
even though my journey
was supposed to be short.
Sometimes I liked to travel
for fun on my days off
and sometimes
I didn't want to see an airplane.
I had to deal with passengers
who got drunk at the airline club,
and would grab my butt
as I pushed the cart down the aisle.
I dealt with their frustrations
due to being hassled by the TSA,
yelled at by gate agents
or dealing with constant delays
and cancellations due to weather

or mechanical problems.
Often passengers missed their connections.
The seats got narrower and the legroom lessened.
The planes got smaller so the seats sold out faster.
The ticket prices got higher
because of five airline mergers
within the last thirteen years.
It got harder to redeem miles.
The airlines started charging passengers for everything.
Sometimes my passengers
didn't get off of their phones
even when we were ready to depart,
got up to get their bags out of the bin
the second the plane lifted off of the ground,
changed diapers on the seats,
and allowed their children
to run around the plane, scream
and kick other passengers in the back
while they watched movies and slept.
Some did yoga in the galley.

Over the years I stopped smiling,
I often took my frustration
towards the company
out on the passengers
even though I shouldn't have.
I missed spending
the holidays with family.
I only stayed
because I had to put
my kids through college.
But I lasted thirty years.

# Hair, the Sequel, 1992-2019

It's an important issue
as you can see
As I continued my hair journey
from pixie cut to hip length
after I wrote my first poem
about hair in the summer of 1992,
I got a blunt cut
to even out the length that November
It reached my shoulders
I was a sophomore in high school
It rained a lot that school year,
so I got relaxers put in
and started using heat tools
as my hair was frizzy all of the time
My hair reached my waist
by the time I entered
my senior year of high school
Then it started to break off
from relaxers, too much heat
and the way I was brushing it
By the time I graduated high school
it only reached my collarbone
and was extremely damaged
I should have gotten another pixie cut to start over
but I didn't want really short hair again
It remained damaged for ten years,

not growing past my shoulder blades
and going through more relaxers
and one highlighting treatment in 2002,
which my hair hated from the start
It felt like straw
As I was about to enter
my second year of graduate school in 2004
I got it cut to the base of my neck
I ate better, took vitamins,
moisturized it and didn't use heat or relaxers
It reached my hips by the end of 2007
Then I started having it relaxed again
in May of 2013
I don't know why I did that
It gradually began to get extremely damaged again
I started transitioning to natural at the end of 2015
by studying hair tutorials on YouTube,
going through a trial and error period with products,
and making homemade hair masques
of olive oil, avocado and honey
I also cut way back on the heat
and eliminated relaxers altogether
I got the damage cut into the shape
of a short-layered bob
for my late maternal grandmother's
100th birthday party
in June of 2017
Frustrated that my hair only grew
from the base of my neck
to right below my collarbone
within the last two years
I decided to get a blunt bob cut
in September 2019
Now I am not sure
I want to grow it really long again
as I love this new cut

but I will continue with my quarterly trims,
use my home made deep conditioner,
take my vitamins,
and continue to eat right and drink a lot of water
all while maintaining my habit
of pretty much leaving my hair alone

# "The Change": Growing Up Part Three

*(Sequel to Growing Up)*

My first "Growing Up" poem
was written when I was twelve years old
and at the beginning stages of adolescence
Now, thirty years later, I am forty-two
and at the beginning stages of perimenopause
It reminds me of puberty a lot
The acne,
the mood swings,
people getting on my nerves,
feeling angry,
keeping up with new changes
and learning how to deal with them
It's called the "puberty of middle age"
or "The Change"

At the beginning of puberty
to look more grown up
I got my ears pierced
and dressed up most every day
I noticed labels and logos for the first time
on gifts and hand-me-downs made by Guess, Gap and DKNY
Although my susceptibility to brand names continues
now my main thing is to be comfortable

by wearing loose cotton tee shirts, dresses
or as sweatpants
as I experience hot flashes
that last for minutes
and come with rashes,
a flushed face,
an increased heart rate
and irritability
Afterwards come the cold flashes
where I shiver for a few minutes
because I lost so much body heat
I try not to overload myself with blankets
when going to sleep, and dress in all-cotton sleepwear
because night sweats interrupt my sleep

Now my eyes get dry or watery
I get a fuzzy brain
My skin feels too dry,
and seems more sensitive,
so I eat anything that has a probiotic,
use a lot of lotion
and take vitamins
targeted at preventing thinning hair
in an effort to keep the full head of hair that I have
I also tend to carry more water weight
Even my hands and feet get swollen
My OB/GYN says,
"Calcium, calcium, calcium,"
a regimen that I have been on
since I was thirty
when they found stress-fractures
in my low back
I don't want to be any shorter
than I already am
Everything I am experienceing relates to estrogen

To reduce my symptoms
I am advised to exercise and practice deep breathing,
which I prefer to medications
The advice is to eat tofu and other soy based foods
plus lots of fruits and vegetables
And avoid eating big meals,
wait for foods to cool when served at really hot temperatures,
abstain from drinking alcohol and anything with caffeine
and never choose spicy foods,
none of which I like, anyway
I have cut way back
on carbs and sugar
to fight the perimenopause belly bulge,
which I had already started
to counter a diagnosis of pre-diabetes
I have to elevate my legs, lessen my salt intake
and drink a lot of water
It's all about the estrogen
Or lack thereof
These adjustments do help

I realize that just like with puberty
when I "celebrated" the beginning of an era,
now I am on the way to celebrating its ending

# Acknowledgements

Many thanks to Carla Blank for editing and Ishmael Reed for his great critical eye and ear.

The following poems first appeared in previous publications:

"Like An Old Friend Whom You Had Given Up for Dead Rain Returns to Oakland" was published in *Alta, Journal of Alta California,* Fall 2019/Issue 9

"California Burning" was published in *Konch Magazine,* Fall 2018

"Spring 2018" was published in *Konch Magazine,* Summer 2018

"You Can't Only Call Them White Nationalists" was published in *Konch Magazine,* Winter 2018

"Hair, the Sequel" and "Ode to the Vegan Poet" were published in *Konch Magazine,* July/August, 2017.

"The Avalanche of Sils im Engadin" and "Mulhouse, France" were published in *American Multiculturalism in Context: Views from at Home and Abroad,* ed. Sämi Ludwig. Newcastle upon Tyne: Cambridge Scholars Publishing, 2017.

"Venice May 2016" and "Why no Flowers for Africa?" were published in *Una Bussola per l'infosfera,* ed. Nicola Paladin and Giorgio Raimondi, Milan: Agenzia X, 2017.

"Wednesday, November 9, 2016" was published in *Konch Magazine*, December, 2016.

"How High the Moon" was published in *Black Renaissance Noir*, May, 2015.

"Spike the Iguana" was published in *Konch Magazine*, September/October 2014.

"Family Feud" was published in *Artists Against Attacks on Gaza*, August 2014.

"*L.R. Californicus*" was published in *The East Bay Review*, June 2014.

"The Ethnic Blues" was published in *Konch Magazine*, May 2014.

"Swimming" was published in *Konch Magazine*, March/April of 2014.

"Miami: A Mural" was published in *Konch Magazine*, April of 2013.

"The Two Friendly Geese" was published in *Konch Magazine*, February of 2013.

"Mid-Afternoon Brain Freeze" was published in *Konch Magazine*, January 2013 and *Fightin' Words: 25 Years of Provocative Poetry and Prose from "The Blue Collar PEN"* (Heyday, 2014).

# About the Author

TENNESSEE REED IS a writer, editor, photographer and videographer. She began writing as a child. Her first poetry collection, *Circus in the Sky* (I. Reed Books, 1988), was published when she was eleven years old, and consists of poems she wrote between the ages of five and eleven. The poems in her second collection, *Electric Chocolate* (Raven's Bones Press, 1990), were written between the ages of eleven and thirteen. Her third collection, *Airborne* (Raven's Bones Press, 1996), was written from ages thirteen through nineteen. Her fourth and fifth books, *City Beautiful* and *Animals & Others*, are combined in *City Beautiful, Poems 1998-2006*, (Ishmael Reed Publishing Company, 2006), a collection written from her third year in college through graduate school, into 2006. Her most recent poetry collection is *New and Selected Poems, 1982-2011* (World Parade Books, 2011).

Tennessee Reed's poetry has also appeared in the *San Francisco Examiner*, the journals *Quilt, California State Library Foundation Bulletin, Poetry USA* nos. 25 and 26, *The Raven Chronicles, Konch, Black Renaissance Noire, counterpunch.org*; and included in the anthologies *From Totems to Hip Hop*, edited by Ishmael Reed (Thunder's Mouth Press, 2003), *Fightin' Words: 25 Years of Provocative Poetry and Prose from "The Blue Collar PEN* (2014), edited by Judith Cody, Kim McMillon and Claire Ortalda, *American Multiculturalism in Context, Views from at Home and Abroad* (2017), edited by Sämi Ludwig, and *una bussola per l'infosfera* (A Compass for the Infosphere, 2017), edited by Giorgio Rimondi and Nicola Paladin.

Tennessee Reed's memoir, *Spell Albuquerque: Memoir of a "Difficult" Student*, was published by CounterPunch Press and AK Press in 2009. An excerpt was published in June 2002 on the internet site of the National Council of Teachers of English. Her novel, *Adventures Among the X Challenged*, was published by Ishmael Reed Publishing Company in 2013. Her essay, "Being Mixed in America," appears in *MultiAmerica: Essays on Cultural Wars and Cultural Peace*, edited by Ishmael Reed (Viking, 1997), and was first published in *The Baltimore Sun* (April 1995). Still in manuscript she currently has a children's book, *The Troll and the Magical Music Box*, and two short stories, "Cloud City," and "The Remember Woman of Una," which also became a one act play performed by the author in 2009.

Tennessee Reed has presented her writing in public readings and on radio and TV since the age of eight. These engagements occurred throughout the mainland United States, Alaska, Hawaii, England, the Netherlands, Spain, Germany, Switzerland, Italy, Israel and Japan. Music for her poems "Old Parents Blues," composed by Carman Moore, and "Three Heavens and Hells," composed by Meredith Monk, which she recorded on *Volcano Songs* (ECM New Series, 1997) and continues to perform, was premiered at the East Bay Dance Series in 1992, as part of a live performance project by The Children's Troupe of Roberts + Blank, of which Ms. Reed was a member.

She also began taking photographs as a child. From 2007, with the improvements in digital technology, she started concentrating on this form, adding videography in 2013. Her photographs have appeared in *The New York Times, The Wall Street Journal, The Buffalo Evening News, The Huffington Post, Berkeleyside, Haaretz, El Pais, WORD*, an anthology of *A Gathering of the Tribes* (2017), on the cover of *Killing Trayvons: An Anthology of American Violence* (2014), illustrating *Storming the Old Boys' Citadel: Two Pioneer Women Architects of Nineteenth*

*Century North America* (2014) and as other authors' photos on various book jackets.

Tennessee Reed was born and raised in Oakland, California, where she continues to make her home. She serves as chairperson of PEN Oakland and is managing editor of the online international literary magazine, *Konch*.